Heroes And Haunts Of The Great Lakes © 2013 by Bruce Jenvey

Published by
Coven Books
Royal Oak, MI 48067
www.covenbooks.com
Cover Art © 2013 by Bruce Jenvey

D1277434

Heroes And Haunts
Of The Great Lakes
By Bruce Jenvey

Dedication

This book is for *all* the people of the Great Lakes Region, whose tenacity, ingenuity and imagination have always put them a cut above, and a step ahead. It is both for those who have left their mark on our heritage, and for those yet to come...

Foreword

For ten years, I had the distinct pleasure of exploring the Great Lakes Region as a journalist. Every month, I wrote about this place or that, sharing my findings of better inns, choice restaurants and favorite attractions, all in hopes of making someone else's journey to these shores as enjoyable as possible.

Along the way, I discovered some truly wonderful stories of local history that just never seem to make the history books. These were inspiring stories of heroes, innovators and great battles, on both land and sea. There were tales of humor and lessons learned as well as little known legends and the stories of local haunts.

I shared these stories, every month, in the pages of Great *Lakes Cruiser Magazine*, and now, I am very pleased to share them with you, here. These are my personal favorites, the stories, the tales and the legends that are all a part of my own Great Lakes Heritage. And now, they are a part of yours, too. Enjoy...

The Great Canal Race Of 1871

With a title like this, I'll bet you're waiting to read about steamships racing for local glory along a limited waterway. Well, you're wrong. This race was between a canal that didn't exist and a train from Kansas. It involves the Army Corps Of Engineers, the populations of two cities and a very important piece of paper. It is perhaps one of the strangest stories of life in the Great Lakes and one that reminds us all, to never underestimate the power of a people united. Intrigued? You should be!

It was the spring of 1871. In those days, the only way into the Superior, Wisconsin—Duluth, Minnesota harbor was through the Superior Entrance across the great sandbar at the mouth of the St. Louis River. Of course, this put the Superior docks in line for the waterborne commerce first, and made it a difficult trip up the harbor to the docks in Duluth. To improve their economic situation, the people of Duluth decided to carve their own canal through the sandbar near Little Portage along the north edge of Minnesota Point.

Of course, the folks in Superior, Wisconsin didn't like that much. Not only would it end their monopoly on the commerce, there was great fear that such a canal would change the course of the St. Louis River enough to cause the Superior Entrance to silt itself closed. The north end of the harbor was shallow, swampy and contained several floating, bog islands. If the river exited here, surely the bogs and swamps would reform in the southern, the Superior end, of the harbor. The people of Superior even enlisted the help of the Army Corps Of Engineers who quickly conducted a study that supported that fear.

But still, the people of Duluth pressed on with their plans. In response, the people of Superior took the matter to the highest authority; Army Headquarters at Fort Leavenworth, Kansas. The Army Court issued an injunction against the City Of Duluth from dredging a new canal and dispatched the all important piece of paper by train to be properly served by an officer of the court. In those days, physically serving the injunction was a legal requirement.

But in 1871, words could travel faster than trains thanks to the telegraph lines. When the people of Duluth received word that the injunction was on its way, they made one of the most important decisions in Great Lakes history: The injunction prevented them from dredging a "new" canal... but what if a navigable canal already existed when the injunction arrived? It would be a different story then!

The decision was made to mobilize the population of Duluth. The train was coming and it would be a race to complete a canal before it arrived. As the story goes, church bells rang and the town closed down. Every man, woman and child mustered at the great sandbar with every digging utensil to be had. They worked without rest and with the help of the river currents and the natural forces of water, they broke through to the big lake and let the mighty St. Louis carry the swampy silt and the bog islands out of the harbor and into deep water.

When the man with the injunction arrived in Duluth on April 29, 1871, he was met by a very dirty, but enthusiastic crowd that lined the banks of a yet uncharted canal. It was only 40-feet wide and 5-feet deep but the crowd cheered as the tugboat *Frank C. Fero*, steamed through the canal into the harbor. This navigation canal was pre-existing to the injunction, making the court order worthless.

Despite continued opposition from the people of Superior, the Duluth canal was improved and expanded to its current size of 300 feet wide. Yes, its *current* size. If you entered this harbor under the famous Aerial Bridge, you traveled through this very canal dug by the men, the women and the children of Duluth. And the Superior Entrance? It seems the Army Corps Of Engineers was wrong. The entrance never silted up and the bogs never formed in the south. This too, is the same entrance that is still in use today. Like I told you, *never* underestimate the power of a people united!

The Boy From Port Huron

Here's a story from Port Huron, Michigan. Port Huron is a small city at the most southern end of Lake Huron at the head of the St. Clair River which has made it a shipping and railroad hub for many years. A tremendous amount of goods, products and people have found their way through this city, all on their way to bigger and better things. This is one of those stories.

If you visit the local Visitors and Convention Bureau there, you'll find it located in the old railroad depot at the foot of the Blue Water Bridge in a beautiful park-like setting. There's lots of helpful information there, but you can't shake the feeling that something important also happened here. Just outside, across the street there's a statue. It's not the likeness of some old stuffy guy on a horse or other typical statue. It's a statue of a very young man, wearing a railroad cap and carrying what looks like a bundle of newspapers.

A very long time ago, this young man lived in Port Huron. He didn't have the greatest childhood. In the fourth grade, he was dismissed from school and labeled "addled brained and unteachable." His mother taught him herself, the best she could at home. At a young age, he went to work for the railroad, in fact, working out of that same old depot just across the street. He was less than a model employee. He was sometimes late, and was often caught in the baggage car printing his own newspaper he sold on the train, or playing with a small chemistry set in a lab he had built on a back table. In short, while he seemed to be industrious, he never seemed to be *where* he was supposed to be, doing *what* he was supposed to be doing.

One day, the train hit a pretty rough piece of track and the chemistry set hit the printing press and it started a fire. While they got it under control pretty quickly, it was the end of the railroad career for this young man. At the age of 16, he left Port Huron and moved on to make his way in the world.

Actually, he did pretty well. You see, that addled-brained, unteachable, lazy, careless, young boy, was none other than Thomas Alva Edison and he went on to invent the phonograph, the light bulb and something called moving pictures among *many* other things.

One of the greatest inventive geniuses in all of history, was born in Ohio, grew up in Port Huron, Michigan and was once fired for nearly burning down a train…

So Why Did They Build Fayette?

Fayette, Michigan is a genuine 'ghost town' located in the western end of the Upper Peninsula on Lake Michigan's northern shoreline. It's a short drive east of Escanaba near the far end of the Garden Peninsula so it's a little off the beaten path and also a little out of your way… but well worth the effort. This abandoned company town is now a State Park and preserves a brief but interesting period in our Great Lakes heritage.

Fayette was a tremendously successful industrial complex in the mid-1800s, built as a remote outpost on the fringes of civilization. Why do this? Why build Fayette here? In order to understand the reasons, you have to understand the demands and limitations of the era.

Prior to the Civil War, Michigan's Upper Peninsula was already established as a source for top grade iron ore. The first lock at Sault Ste. Marie was put into operation in 1855, primarily to ease the shipping hassles of unloading and re-loading this valuable cargo from ship to ship around the Saint Mary's Rapids. All railroad development and route planning centered around delivering iron ore from the mining operation to where ever it might be needed. Iron ore was king, and everything revolved around its development.

When the War Between The States broke out, demand for iron products increased dramatically and the Jackson Iron Company (the "Company" of Fayette) foresaw a great demand for their product both during the war and the inevitable period of reconstruction that would follow. The Company's board of directors approved the construction of an Upper Peninsula blast furnace and purchased some of their first land on the Garden Peninsula before the war was even over. But why up there?

Remember, what Industrial America needed was high grade iron, not iron ore, to build the machines that would take us into the 20th century. Raw iron ore contains a number of impurities that adds to its weight and volume and when you pay your shipper by weight and volume, it adds to the cost of your final product. It would be more economically feasible to refine the iron ore up there, and pay the shipping costs to the factories of the industrial cities on only that portion you were going to use anyway. This was one reason but by no means, the principal or deciding factor. It was the technology of the day that made Fayette economically feasible.

Iron ore is smelted in blast furnaces. These furnaces take their names from the blasts of
heated air driven into the combustion chambers in order to raise the internal temperatures as high as possible. The hotter the furnace, the more complete the smelting process rendering a higher quality end product. The hottest blast furnaces of this era burned charcoal, a technological limitation.

Yes, there were blast furnaces in the industrial cities like Chicago, Detroit and Cleveland, but they burned coal or coke as their source of fuel and therefore produced a product inferior to anyone running a charcoal blast furnace. So why didn't they burn charcoal?

Charcoal is relatively light when compared to its bulk. It also absorbs water quite quickly and can easily become ruined beyond use in the presence of relatively small amounts of water. If you want to prove it to yourself, invite the neighbors over for a BBQ but hit the Kingsford with the garden hose first.

These factors made it a fuel that didn't transport well in the holds of ships traveling the stormy, inland seas called the Great Lakes. And in order to make your own charcoal locally, you had to have a large supply of quality hardwood trees close at hand. Unfortunately, anything that resembled a tree in these large industrial metropolises had long since been cleared away. There were no significant stands of timber within a reasonable distance to make charcoal blast furnaces economically feasible. However, coal was plentiful, its weight ratio made it a much more practical fuel to transport and by nature, it was much more likely to survive the trip.

Even if the iron that came out of these furnaces was slightly inferior, it was considered "good enough" and in step with the competition.

And then one day in 1867, Fayette Brown, agent for the Jackson Iron Company sailed into what was then called Snail Shell Harbor. He found a deep, perfectly protected harbor large enough to accommodate the bulk carrying schooners of the day. It was only a few miles by water from Escanaba where the Company had recently completed the railroad line that ran directly to their iron ore mines. The entire area was covered with high quality Michigan hardwood trees that would be perfect for the local production of charcoal. The final needed ingredient, a flux to bond with the impurities during the smelting process was readily at hand too. The great limestone cliffs that protected the harbor were only part of the large natural deposit of this stone on the peninsula. On top of all that, the land was cheaper here than in any industrial city or in the mining district to the North. After all, what value could the land have? There was no iron ore
here!

Within minutes of seeing the harbor, Fayette Brown had purchased the land from a local farmer who found this portion impossible to plow what with all the limestone just inches below the surface. Construction started the same year and by 1870, two full blast furnaces and an entire society existed here. Several times during the twenty some years of its productive life, this facility out produced everyone in the business, and was well known throughout the industrial harbors of the Great Lakes. So what brought about the demise of such a naturally successful community? Technology.

As the late 19th century approached, iron ore smelting technology progressed to the point where coal and coke burning furnaces could equal and then surpass the smelting temperatures of charcoal furnaces. With this breakthrough, the scales shifted very quickly and it became much more profitable to smelt in the industrial cities than back in Fayette.

In 1891, the Jackson Iron Company disassembled their machinery and moved on. Most of the workers dispersed to other jobs in the peninsula area immediately leaving Fayette nearly abandoned. The hotel hung on for some time serving the resort crowd but it too eventually closed its doors. The Catholic Church up on the hill managed to remain in operation until it burned in 1972 and was never rebuilt. The main portion of the town was acquired by the
State Of Michigan in 1959 and fortunately for all of us, some said "What a great place for a State Park…"

Iron Men & Wooden Ships
The Story Of The Langell Shipyard

One of the most famous industries to ever call St. Clair, Michigan home, is now but a footnote in history. Gone, and to many people, nearly forgotten. But if you're staying on a boat in the marina, this piece of history is close at hand. You just have to look around you... or below you, for a possible trace or a glimpse into the past. If you still can't see it, I encourage you to visit the St. Clair Historical Commission Museum located in the old Baptist Church on South Fourth Street. They can give you more than a glimpse, they can show you maps and photographs of the famed, Langell Brothers Shipyard. In preparing this story, I was most fortunate to have the help of the museum which allowed access to a narrative written by William Langell in 1934. History this good, needs to be repeated!

Captain Simon Langell was born in Nova Scotia in 1835, the son of French Huguenot refugees who fled France during the revolution. When Simon was only eight years old, his father moved the family to Newport, Michigan, a small town on the St. Clair River known better today as Marine City.

Simon struggled to educate himself and eventually secured a teacher's certificate. But after a short while, the shipyards of Marine City called louder than the classrooms of rural Michigan. Simon Langell began building boats, at first for others, and then for himself further north in St. Clair.

In 1878, Captain Langell moved his shipyard from the shallow waters of the St. Clair River bank just south of the Pine River, to property just inside the first bend of the Pine River on the south bank, a site today occupied by the public boat harbor and the adjacent private boating facility. The marina's horseshoe pit stands approximately where the bow end of some of the Great Lakes' finest schooners and steamers took shape.

Ship building in those days was a rugged business. Huge wooden beams were roughed-in by hand-axe and cut to size with hand-operated whip saws. Holes for structural supports were augured into the wood, by hand. Who built these ships? Half of the Langell Brothers yard crew were French-Canadians from Montreal and Quebec who had built ships for the very demanding British. The other half were Scottish immigrants… who had also built ships for the British. These two groups rivaled each other as to who could build the toughest, the fastest... you get the idea. The bottom line is that some of the finest ships ever built came out of this yard and commerce on the Great Lakes was the true benefactor of their labor. These were definitely, as William Langell himself said, "Iron men building wooden ships."

Some of the more famous ships to leave these ways included the *Fontana* and the *Kaliyuga*. In their days, each was rated the best wooden ship on the water. The *Kaliyuga* was also the largest ship the Langells ever built at 1,941 tons. The entire town turned out for her christening in 1887. But shipping in those days before radio and weather radar was a dangerous profession. The *Kaliyuga* was lost with all hands in the teeth of a Lake Huron gale, in 1905.

The steamer *Langell Boys* also deserves mention here because of the name she bore and because she was built for the use by the Langells themselves. She met her end, as so many wooden steamers did, by fire. A blaze started in the engine compartment and overtook the ship on Saginaw Bay. While there was no loss of life, the *Langell Boys* burned to the waterline and sank before anyone could help her.

I once heard an old man near the Soo telling stories to young boys about the early days of shipping on the lakes and the vast number of steamers lost to fire. "When you start building fires inside wooden boats and then tossin' 'em about on the likes of these Great Lakes, well... you're bound to singe the carpet now and then…"

By the turn-of-the-century, steel boats were the preferred construction method and the iron men who built the wooden ships faded into the history books.

History Of A Hymn

History comes to all things and more often than not, takes unusual twists, turns, and encounters with fate. Such is the story of one of our culture's most famous Christian hymns, "What A Friend We Have In Jesus." Everybody knows that one. But what you don't know is the unusual story behind its creation, a story, I am going to tell you, backwards!

The hymn can be credited, in part, to Charles Converse of the Converse Organ Factory in Pennsylvania. He wrote the music anyway, but the inspiring words? He found them on the floor of his factory. There they were, one ordinary day about 1870, on a scrap of newspaper someone had accidentally left behind. Converse was so inspired by those words, he sat right down and set them to music on one of his brand new organs.

But how did these inspiring words come to be there where Converse would find them? Earlier that day, a traveling music salesman had visited the floor of the factory and would later admit he was quite distraught when he lost his only copy of this most beautiful poem.

But where did *he* get them? He had found them published in a New York newspaper and was so touched by the words, he cut them out and carried them with him. So where did the newspaper get them? Someone brought the poem to the paper on yet another piece of paper. It seems this particular New Yorker had received a present from a friend in the mail. The present was wrapped in newspaper from the sender's hometown. Exposed and intact, were the now famous words to this hymn.

So how did this other newspaper get them? That's the *start* of this story. The newspaper that was used as gift wrapping was the *Port Hope Guide*, a small newspaper from a small town just east of Toronto, along the Lake Ontario shoreline. They had published this original poem, "What A Friend We Have In Jesus," by a local scholar and lay preacher named Joseph Mendlicott Scriven.

Scriven had emigrated to Port Hope from Dublin, Ireland in 1845. He had lived in the cottage areas around nearby Rice Lake before eventually moving into the village itself. Scriven died in 1886, well-known locally as a humanitarian but other than that, an obscure but kindly man who gave his all to a community. Yet he is the man who wrote the words, that were published in the paper, that was used as gift wrap, that were republished in New York, that were cut out by the music salesman that were lost on the floor of the organ factory in Pennsylvania.

While Scriven is buried on the north shore of Rice Lake, a monument inscribed with his famous words stands today in the northeast corner of Port Hope's Memorial Park.

America's Kitchen Tables

Rochester, New York has always been known as a center for innovation and invention. In fact, Greater Rochester had the distinction of being the "Patent Capital of the World," until only recently when it was finally eclipsed by the Silicon Valley. On a per-capita basis, more patents were issued to citizens of Greater Rochester than anyplace else on Earth. That's quite a distinction, and they held that title for well over a century.

What great ideas came out of Rochester? Well, the fountain pen for one, baby shoes for another. It was early in the community's history that an inventive young woman revolutionized the ladies undergarment industry. Her name was Amelia Bloomer. In 1853, two immigrants got together and established the town's first optical store. These two guys were none other than John Bausch and Henry Lomb… the rest is history. But wait, there's more! In 1895, someone from Rochester with a bit of whimsy gave the world marshmallows, and just two years later, someone else gave us our first taste of Jell-O.

In 1906 a small office supply company opened above a Rochester shoe factory. The Haloid Company nearly went bankrupt three times, but hung in there. In 1959, they finally hit on a breakthrough idea that would allow businesses to re-create their most important documents quickly. Two years later, Haloid changed its name to… Xerox.

So what's all this got to do with Kitchen tables? Lots. An amazing number of these inventions and corporations were founded on ideas that came off the kitchen table, either before or after dinner. None more exemplifies this uniquely American process than my last example of a young bank teller named George.

George lived at home with his mother and worked in the bank every day. In the evenings, after dinner, he liked to play around with photography. Back in his day, photography was a very involved process and the kitchen table was the only place he could spread out his professional paraphernalia. But the more he played with the process, the more he became confident that he could simplify it… even to the point where complete amateurs could start taking pictures.

In 1888, he did it, and brought his first camera for the common man to the marketplace. Sales were phenomenal and Mr. Eastman was *very* successful. Did I forget to mention? That bank teller was none other than George Eastman and right there on that kitchen table, between the roast beef and the applesauce, the Eastman-Kodak Company was born. It still calls Rochester home today, but the facilities are a bit nicer.

This should be both proof and inspiration to all that America's best ideas don't necessarily start on the drawing board in some fancy lab, or in some far away conference room. Sometimes, the best ideas start right at the kitchen table and create their *own* opportunity.

Ghosts And Speed Demons

While this title sounds like something that should have made our Halloween issue, I assure, you, these are friendly ghosts. This is a story of modern achievement and technical advancement and ironically, it starts in a time we all consider to be, "the olden days."

In May, 1861, the Civil War had barely begun. There were no electric lights, no telephones and the highest technological achievement of the day was the steam locomotive. Yet, on the 20th day of that month, in that time, a Mr. & Mrs. Smith of rural St. Clair County, Michigan, were blessed with a son they named, Christopher Columbus. He was one of the younger children in the family and in his mid-teen years, he dropped out of school (by now the family had moved into the nearby village of Algonac) to join his older brother Henry in the "market hunting" business.

Market hunting meant these two outdoorsmen spent all day, every day, out in the marshes and backwaters of the St. Clair Flats, hunting ducks… several hundred a week, in order to keep fine game food on the tables of Detroit's better restaurants. In short order, young Christopher became a crack shot and a legendary, duck decoy carver. In order to increase their take in the fields, the boys resorted to the use of duck boats to navigate the Flats and carry their game. Being hunters of simple means, they had to build their own duck boats and if you're going to build your own, why not build it your own way?

The two Smith brothers had earned quite a reputation in the area as skilled hunters with a great knowledge of the Flats. It was not uncommon for them to act as guides for recreational hunters from time to time. And when these city hunters got a ride in one of the Smith's duck boats, they started placing orders!

Over time, the Smiths were spending more time building duck boats than they were hunting. This seemed to suit Chris but Henry preferred his outdoorsman way of life. Eventually he left the budding boat building business and went back to the marshes of the Flats, but not before he had helped his brother turn a page in history.

Steam launches used as tour boats were all the rage in the very late 1800s. But steam engines were bulky, hot, smelly and reasonably dangerous to sit next to. A slight improvement over this system was the naphtha engine, which worked much like a steam engine, but used naphtha instead of water as the expanding component. Fascinated by this concept, the boys saved their money and bought one of these naphtha engines and somehow, managed to mount it in one of their larger rowboats. It worked! They took turns and sold rides aboard this "wonder craft" as it raced up and down the St. Clair River at four or five miles an hour!

What was so remarkable about this was that these engines were all designed for larger, commercial launches. The Smith brothers had put one in a personal-size watercraft that anyone could own and operate. In another similar twist of fate, a local gentleman had purchased one of those new-fangled gasoline engines from a Grand Rapids manufacturer. He could never get it to work right and soon became frustrated. He sold the engine to the Smiths who tinkered with it joyously, but less than successfully.

One day, the manufacturer showed up in Algonac with something he felt would make it run better: a carburetor. Sure enough, the gasoline engine soon lived up to its promises as a smaller, more powerful engine system that could drive anything attached to it, better and faster. Chris was hooked, but Henry had had enough and went back to hunting in the Flats.

Christopher Columbus Smith was earning quite a reputation for himself as a quality boat builder and the "fastest man in the Flats" when he met "Baldy" Ryan. Ryan was a St. Louis gambler and financier who had built a summer home in the Algonac area. After watching one of Chris' boats, *The Dart* race up and down the river at just over 20 mph with its smiling owner, Ryan commissioned the C.C. Smith Boat Company to build one for *him* that could beat it.

It was Ryan who started taking Christopher Smith boats (not yet, Chris-Craft) to organized sporting and racing events and soon became a partner in the business. Chris would build the boats, Ryan and Chris' son Jay W. Smith would race them and everybody would want to buy one. The boat business prospered and Ryan took the reputation of the Algonac boat builder to the highest levels of international racing before a life of excess finally caught up with Baldy Ryan. He was a gambler and a high roller and no matter how much money your business makes, some things just roll the wrong way and shortly after 1910, Baldy Ryan found himself personally bankrupt. The partnership was dissolved and try as he might, the Smiths just
could not keep the racing syndicate going on their own.

Enter, Gar Wood, Garfield Arthur Wood. He had become addicted to the smell of gasoline and the rush of water while still a lightning rod salesman in the Midwest. It followed him through his days as a manufacturer (he had invented an unloading device for dump trucks) right up to the moment he bought the battered hull of the *Miss Detroit* at a luncheon auction, the very event that the Smiths thought was the end of their racing days. But Gar Wood learned a lot from the boat and soon came to Chris Smith with some ideas and money of his own. That began a racing dynasty that brought the Gold Cup to Detroit.

For several years, Chris Smith was building the fastest boats in the world and Gar Wood and Jay W. were claiming victory after victory, many right there on the Detroit River in front of the Detroit Yacht Club where they still race the unlimited hydroplanes today. It was a good team. While most people were still figuring out how to get gasoline engines to run, dependably, these two were modifying aircraft engines and developing new hull designs that would let them skip across the surface of the water at record setting speeds. Most of those boats were tested and many of those records were set on the St Clair River along the Algonac shoreline.

But people grow in different directions. By 1921, personal differences had driven a wedge between Gar Wood and the Smiths. And while there would be more racing for both, it would not be together and the days of the unbeatable dynasty were over.

But the Smiths did well. Chris and his children went on building a number of performance boats for show and lots of boats for the pleasure crowd. During the 1920s, they moved from downtown Algonac to the facility they built on the west end of the village along
the North Channel, today known as the Harbour Club Marina. Classic, mahogany runabouts and cruisers splashed into the water here, and the name Chris Craft became a legend of the pleasure boating industry.

They say on quiet nights in Algonac, you can still hear the scream of Curtis aircraft engines coming from the river or the smell of Chris' cigar smoke wafting through the Harbour Club. Don't think of these as ghosts, but as gifts... memories of "the fastest man in the Flats."

For more in-depth reading on the history of this unique, boat-building family, let me recommend *The Legend Of Chris Craft* by Jeffery L. Rodengen. It is a wonderfully well-written and complete history of these remarkable people with so very many rare, historical photos. It's available at better book stores everywhere and many gifts shops in the Algonac area.

Cruise Night In Pultneyville

As a journalist, I feel it my duty to warn you about a roving band of ruffians that terrorizes the hamlet of Pultneyville, New York along the southern shore of Lake Ontario. They have no official name, but generally respond to 'The Pultneyville Antique Car Club.' They meet up in the dirt parking lot behind The Pultneyville Pickle, the local snack and ice cream emporium, on any given Tuesday evening in the summertime just as the good, honest folk are getting home from work. After a short time spent admiring each other's clutches and carburetors, they take off through the streets of town and out across the county roads, belching smoke, grinding gears and honking 'augha' horns at innocent passersby. I can speak fully of this, because I have seen it firsthand. Yea, I was their captive, their hostage, one evening and taken places and forced to see things I dare not speak of here... Okay, I will!

I came to Pultneyville to do a feature story for my magazine about this small hamlet's history during the war of 1812, and at the same time, investigate one of its local haunted legends. (This would be for the Halloween issue.) I arrived in town earlier than I planned and decided to spend some time getting familiar with the local geography and scouting some potential photo shots for the next morning when the official Town Historian, Chester Peters, would be along to guide me. On about my third pass by the Pultneyville Pickle, I noticed a small gathering of obviously antique cars forming in the back lot. To me, antique cars are like cheese to the mouse, the flame to the moth. So I pulled in and parked my car at the end of the line.

I grabbed my camera and started to snap a few shots of these choice vehicles when the seemingly pleasant group of owners surrounded me. Getting some of them to pose with their pride and joy rides wasn't difficult until one of them noticed my shirt. Yes, I was wearing a T-Shirt with the Magazine's logo as I often did on 'travel days.' It was one of the women who noticed it first. She pointed a finger at me and shouted:

"You're the magazine guy!"

"What magazine guy?" shouted back one of the men.

"The one that's coming to meet my father tomorrow! That's him!" Yes, it seems Chester Peters' own daughter had fallen in with this nefarious group.

I was not prepared for what happened next. It seemed that picture-taking time was suddenly over and the gang was about to take it on the lam. They lined up to form what would be a fast moving (oh, 25 or 30 mile per hour) caravan of cars representing several decades of American automotive history.

"Enjoy your ride!" I naively waved. But they would have none of that.

"You're coming with us!" they demanded and I was *forced* into the passenger seat of a 1913 Ford Model T Coupe. We took off around the corner onto Washington Street with my get-away driver, Craig, waving at pedestrians, (there were two) and squeezing that huge rubber bulb on the horn of that classic automobile.

I have been a member of the Henry Ford Museum/Greenfield Village for well over thirty years. I have seen such cars as were in this caravan many times before. But in all honesty, I had never ridden in one until this warm September evening. What a rush!

The windshield was open as we wheeled past farm fields and I could smell nearby Lake Ontario in the air. Craig explained the mysterious set of pedals to me as he constantly adjusted the throttle and advanced the spark lever. I have always considered myself fairly well-versed on automotive history, but in the time I spent talking with Craig, I learned a lot I never knew. I guess the advertising slogans of the day were right: "Just ask the man that owns one!"

Here's an interesting tidbit I'll bet you didn't know: In 1913, Henry Ford proclaimed that Americans could have a Ford in any color they wanted, as long as it was black. I had always thought that *all* his cars were black up to that point and that this famous quote was his comment on refusing to expand his color choices. But no! In reality, according to Craig, Model Ts had been available in up to four colors to that date. However, 1913 was the year Ford's new assembly line system of auto manufacturing went into full swing. All those fancy colors took too long to dry and slowed the line down. But the flat back paint he was using dried very quickly, so quickly in fact that the car was ready to be worked on again by the time it reached the next stage in the line. In the interest of building cars cheaper by building them faster, Ford limited the color selection to black only. Imagine how embarrassing it was for this old Detroit boy to have to go all the way to Pultneyville, New York to learn that!

Then, the entire caravan pulled off the road onto a two-track trail through a cornfield. I'd seen this scene in the gangster movies and I feared what might be coming next. I was forced out of the Model T… and into the back seat of a 1931 Model A, a true, family-sized, 50-mile-an-hour automobile. This one was complete with running boards and even a bud vase. Here I was in the back of a real gangster-mobile and me without my Tommy Gun. In a flash, we were back on the main road and leading the caravan as I heard all about this car's history from its discovery in an apple orchard to its distinctive window frames marking it as one style of 'A' as opposed to the other. Amazingly, this was a very comfortable automobile and I can see why it was such a major step forward from the Model T. It is still referred to as the car that saved Ford Motor.

There was another stop or two. I got to stand by the side of the road and admire the rumble seat in a 1936 Ford V-8 while someone went back for a gas can to get one of the Ts running again. Then the classic Jeep Bus suffered an electrical failure. By the time these hooligans had passed me from car to car and then returned me to the Pultneyville Pickle (where they forced me to eat two scoops of strawberry ice cream), only three of the seven cars in the caravan had completed the circuit. An unusual turn of events, you ask? No, just Cruise Night in Pultneyville…

Lucky Ladies Of The Lake
Two Of Blind River's Own Ride Out The Tempest Of 1913

In early November, 1913, the worst storm ever in Great Lakes history ravaged ship and shore for nearly five days. When it was over, hundreds were dead and a dozen lake boats had gone to the bottom. A full two dozen more had been blown from their element and sat as useless wrecks along the shore.

The carnage would have been less, certainly, had modern weather equipment been available. Back then, there was nothing that really resembled a weather forecast. The most reliable predictions came out of almanacs which were nothing more than historical averages and were not based on the current position of weather fronts at all. Lake Captains tended to push on, and sail out into uncertain conditions rather than to lose a valuable day of a limited shipping season. The general attitude was that *you can't do anything about the weather, so worry about it when it happens.* "Happening weather" was a tremendous understatement for the great storm of 1913.

This storm's severity still captures the imaginations of those with an interest in Great Lakes Lore. In recent years, two respected meteorologists were still attempting to "solve the puzzle" as to what meteorological events took place by studying the written accounts of eye witnesses from various ports around the lakes. It has been generally accepted that four low pressure cells converged over Lake Huron and joined forces in a freak occurrence. More recent thoughts discount this theory but still offer no concrete model of their own. What ever happened, Southern Lake Huron took the worst of it leaving very few sailors to recount the ferocity of the tempest.

How bad did it get? Again, weather measuring devices were in their infancy or completely nonexistent in that era, but consistent reports put sustained wind speeds in excess of one hundred miles an hour. The ice and snow that accompanied the storm was said to literally "explode" when hitting houses, barns or those foolish enough to venture outside. Windows were destroyed not just by the wind, but by the large objects that were along for the ride. Entire buildings were obliterated by the ice and wind, or by the trees the ice and wind sent as destroyers. Those who could see the water, told of waves that towered above the highest freighters. And this lasted for five days!

As I mentioned, eyewitness accounts of those who experienced this maelstrom from the water are few and far between, and many of those come from ships who were only on the edges of the storm. Blind River, Ontario in northern most Lake Huron was on the edge of the storm and was home to the two ships in this account:

On the evening of Saturday, November 8th, 1913, the storm had not yet made itself felt in the small lumber town of Blind River. Seeing no reason to waste another night in port, Captain W.E. Pierce was preparing to get underway. His vessel, the aging lake steamer, *Ogemaw,* was loaded to the hilt with prime lumber cut from the northern shores of Georgian Bay. As was the practice, once the hold was filled, more lumber was secured to the open deck in an effort to make every trip count the most, financially. But the *Ogemaw* would not be traveling alone. The schooner barge *CA. Filmore* would be in tow, also loaded above her decks.

This lumber-hooker/schooner-barge combination was very common back then. Old sailing vessels, unable to earn a profitable living in competition to steam boats, would serve out the last useful years of their lives in tow behind aging lakers, themselves unable to keep up with the newest "Ladies of the Lakes." However, when run as a combination, they could justify their existence with a modest profit. Sometimes, one steamer would tow several such schooners and one by one, cut them loose off shore from their intended, respective ports. The schooners would then make their way to shore under sail and when empty, rendezvous with their steamer out on the open lake. This way, one steamer could make deliveries to several ports in a fraction of the time even a much newer boat could have done the same job. It made them profitable and kept the ships and their crews employed for a while longer.

But on this evening, it was just the *Ogemaw* and the *Filmore,* both aging hulks with wooden hulls and tired seams that set out for Alpena, Michigan. Within an hour of leaving Blind River, the weather had dramatically changed. The wind had shifted to the northeast and now screeched down on the sterns of the unsuspecting lumber boats. The seas built quickly making it now impossible to turn around and claw their way back home. The seas mauled both vessels, smashing windows and companionways and slowing stripping their decks of the valuable cargo.

After several hours, Captain Pierce feared this storm might be the end of his ship, his barge, or both and began considering his options for survival. Turning around 180^0 in these seas with a barge in tow would be impossible. If he were to cut the barge loose (as was often the practice), it would spell the certain doom of all eight men on the *Filmore.* And to gain what? The odds were still against the *Ogemaw* making that turn on her own. To venture through the Mississagi Straits on the western end of Manitoulin Island as was their original course, was now also suicide. Out on the open lake, this storm would claim both vessels within minutes.

The third option proved to be their salvation. Along the west end-of Manitoulin Island is Meldrum Bay, only a couple compass points to East of their current course. The bay would provide only limited protection with the wind in its current direction, but limited protection was better than what they had now.

It was a struggle against the seas, but Captain Pierce managed to guide both vessels into Meldrum Bay and there, in the relatively calmer waters, he managed to turn into the wind without losing the *Filmore,* and dropped both his anchors. The *Filmore,* still connected by the towing hawser, also dropped both of her anchors and there they planned to ride out the weather.

Captain Pierce kept his engine engaged at "slow ahead" in order to take some of the strain off the ground tackle. But as the storm intensified throughout the day on Sunday, the 9th, he slowly nudged the throttle further and further ahead until the engine was at its maximum. Still, this was not enough to keep the anchors from dragging across the rocky bottom of the bay.

By Sunday evening, Pierce gave in to what he knew he must do and cut the *Filmore* loose. He hoisted anchor and set out on a last ditch effort to return to Blind River. On the open water, he at least stood a chance. Back there in Meldrum Bay, he was sure to be blown upon the rocks and smashed to pieces by the surf. The *Filmore* would have to fend for herself.

Clawing her way back to Blind River proved to be a monumental task for the *Ogemaw*. Ice and snow pelted the vessel without mercy making visibility on that already black night completely impossible. Ice clung to those portions of her superstructure that struggled to stay above the heaving water. The waves ripped at this grand old lady of the lake, and bit by bit, began stripping her of her deckhouse and pilot house.

By the morning of the tenth, the deckhouse was completely gone and not much remained of the pilot house. Several times during the night, the thought to abandon the ship had crossed the Captain's mind, but waves towering ten feet above the deck had made launching the lifeboats impossible. But now, they could see the entrance to Blind River!

By lunchtime, they were secured to a dock and the crew was attempting to salvage what remained of their personal belongings from what remained of the *Ogemaw*. But the Captain pushed for makeshift repairs and by Tuesday afternoon, when Georgian Bay had managed to calm itself slightly, the *Ogemaw* set out on a return to Meldrum Bay and to the aid of the *Filmore*.

By now, they were certain the *Filmore* was in ruins. If she hadn't blown ashore and been dashed on the rocks, surely the strain of riding anchor in this storm would have opened her seams allowing the cold lake water to rush in and take her. Captain Pierce wasn't going back for the *Filmore,* he was going back for survivors.

But to the surprise of all, the *Filmore* was floating and riding her anchors quite well in the seclusion of Meldrum Bay. The *Ogemaw* hitched up her consort and continued on to deliver what remained of their cargo to Alpena before returning to Blind River for Winter and some much needed repairs.

The *Ogemaw* and the *Filmore* continued to sail together out of Blind River for several more seasons before their final retirement. But where ever they went from then on, they were no longer just two tired lumber boats, they were recognized as those two "Survivors" from Blind River.

Can Lelia Come Out And Play?

If you ever find yourself in Cobourg, Ontario, a short distance east of Toronto, I strongly suggest you visit the Chamber of Commerce offices when you first arrive. You'll find them in a small, red brick cottage at 212 King Street West in the heart of town. Not only will you find them to be a very pleasant and helpful group of people, but you'll find their building to be an attraction all in itself. While you're picking up brochures, historical tour maps and museum hours, look around you at the collection of memorabilia that celebrates the life and times of the city's most famous resident: Lelia Marie Koerber.

She was born in one of the front rooms of this very house on November 9th, 1868, the daughter of Anne Henderson of Port Hope, and a temperamental Austrian music teacher named Alexander Koerber. Her father was a very demanding individual that always, eventually alienated all his young pupils, causing the family to relocate on a regular basis. But Lelia Marie was born, baptized and spent her early years right here.

At the age of 14, in 1882, she decided to leave home and pursue a career on the stage. In those days, this was considered a disreputable career and her father demanded she change her name so as not to drag the Koerber heritage through the mud. She complied and after years of limited success, hit it big with the title role in Broadway's *Tillie's Nightmare* in 1910. That role took her to Hollywood and into a series of silent pictures based on the successful play.

In 1927, she starred in *The Callahans And The Murphys* which earned her a role in the critically acclaimed *Anna Christie*. She went on to star in many Hollywood hits into the 1930s including *Tugboat Annie*, but none so famous as the award winning *Min & Bill* for which she won an Oscar.

The house at 212 King Street West is filled with old movie memorabilia celebrating the life of Lelia Marie Koerber… whom you probably remember better as Hollywood's Marie Dressler…

"We Have Met The Enemy..."

There were several reasons and causes for The War of 1812, the so called "second war of independence." However, probably the *real* underlying motivation was the control of the Great Lakes Region, then known as the Northwest Territory. Everyone knew there was a great wealth of natural resources here. This region was rich with lumber, furs, fish, fertile farmlands, semi-precious metals and valuable ore to mine. But the only way to bring these resources to market was by ship, across the Great Lakes. So he who controlled the shipping lanes would win the Northwest Territory... and that was the *real* prize.

In the summer of 1813, the Americans had been at war with the British for a year, and quite frankly, we were losing. The British Navy had blockaded several of our harbors, their Army had made several successful landings on our shores, and on the Great Lakes, they had our Navy pretty well bottled up at Sackets Harbor in eastern Lake Ontario.

All traffic coming down from the upper lakes was controlled by the British from their position in Amherstburg, Ontario, where the Detroit River empties into Lake Erie. Here they had built Fort Malden and a state of the art, shipbuilding and maintenance facility known as The King's Navy Yard. If the Americans could break the British stranglehold here, they could threaten the entire British position in Ontario.

Into this uncertain situation stepped a young naval officer named Oliver Hazard Perry who would rewrite history and change the course of world events before he was finished. Perry was given a small command of men, virtually no supplies and what seemed like an impossible mission: To take control of the shipping lanes on Lake Erie and end British domination of the upper lakes. What happened next has long been held up as a fine example of American ingenuity and determination.

Perry wasn't even a full Naval Captain yet. He took the title of Commodore as he would be in charge of the American fleet on Lake Erie, a fleet that did not yet even exist. The *real* American fleet on the Great Lakes was at Sackets Harbor in eastern Lake Ontario, below Niagara Falls and with no canal yet built; these ships could not reach the upper lakes. So Perry was to be Commodore of a fleet that he had to build himself, on a lake where he had no naval base, and from this non-existent base, his orders were to attack and defeat the most powerful navy in the world. He was literally left to his own devices as he set up camp in the wilderness of Presque Isle, near what is now Erie, Pennsylvania.

With no seasoned lumber at his disposal, Perry came up with a completely outrageous, yet ingenious plan. He would build an entire fleet of ships, twice the size of the British fleet, but all from freshly cut, green wood. While these ships would not last long in the heat of battle, it was Perry's strategy to build them to fight *one* battle and *one* battle only, overwhelming the enemy with superior numbers. Among the several sloops and schooners they built were two battleships… sister ships: The *Lawrence* (named for Perry's mentor and intended as his flagship) and the *Niagara*. They were equipped with lots of firepower.

While Perry was in the process of building these green ships, Captain Barclay, the senior British officer in charge at Amherstburg, twice brought his ships within cannon range of Perry's shipyard in order to 'keep an eye' on him. It was within Barclay's power at that time to open fire and destroy the ships, the yard and the entire American effort on the lake. No one knows why he never took this opportunity. He could have done so in complete safety to his own ships. You see, the British ships were armed with long-range, highly accurate, rifled cannons. The best the Americans had and what they were installing on their green ships were shorter-ranged, less accurate cannonades, but again, Perry had twice as many of these than the British did their cannons.

By mid-summer, the ships were done and Perry took his fragile fleet out into the open lake. He established a base on South Bass Island at Put-In-Bay, knowing from there, he could control shipping on the lake and effectively cut the British supply line. You see, Perry knew he lacked the ships to launch a direct attack on the British stronghold. The water gets shallow around Amherstburg and maneuverability would be at a minimum. Also, the fort was as heavily armed as the British fleet and he knew his greenwood ships would not stand up well in battle. Perry wanted to force Barclay out into the open.

The plan worked. By the end of the summer, the British at the Navy Yard and Fort Malden were on half rations and morale was suffering. Finally, on September 9th, 1813, Barclay was forced to leave the safety of the river and met Perry on his own waters. He led the way himself aboard his flagship, the *H.M.S. Detroit* closely followed by the powerful *Queen Charlotte* and the rest of the fleet. On the morning of the 10th, a lookout in Perry's fleet saw the approaching British and sounded the alarm.

The American Navy had been waiting for this day. Perry, aboard the *Lawrence,* led his fleet into the pending battle. But remember, these were the days when the British all wore red coats and marched in a straight line. They didn't know how to fight the Americans who tended to hide behind rocks and trees and wear colors found in nature. This was also true of their naval tactics. The British liked to line up their ships, stem to stern and fire broadsides at you as they sailed past. They called this, a "line of fire" and no enemy ever, had broken through such a formation.

However, Perry had another idea. Rather than sail side by side with the British as Barclay expected him to do, he used a favorable wind shift and sailed *right at* them! The *Lawrence* led the way with the *Niagara* right behind. The *Lawrence* was shelled without mercy with many casualties and much damage as they closed the distance. This unnerved the British enough, but then Perry did something *really* strange!

As the *Lawrence* was nearly upon the British, nothing much more than a sinking, dying hulk, Perry pulled down his battle standard, boarded his gig and rowed a short distance back to the *Niagara*. He changed ships in the middle of a battle! As the British finally blasted the *Lawrence* out of their way, there they were, face to face with the *Niagara*, fresh, undamaged and blasting from both broadsides. Behind her, was the rest of the American fleet.

The two principle British brigs, the *Detroit* and the *Queen Charlotte* both suffered immediate damage and quickly attempted to change their positions, but in the smoke and the confusion, they collided and entangled their rigging. Helpless, defenseless and directly under the American guns, they surrendered. The rest of the British fleet tried to scatter and flee back to Amherstburg, but the American ships rounded them up and the victory was complete. Oliver Hazard Perry had done what no man had ever done before: He had broken through a British line of fire and then captured their entire fleet!

That night, Perry penned his now famous message to his commanding officer, Army General, William Henry Harrison on the back of an envelope: "We have met the enemy, and they are ours..." What followed was a list of captured ships. You've probably heard this famous phrase before, but never realized that it was coined so close to home.

Barclay's career was now over. When he would eventually reach England again, he would face court-martial charges for his handling of the entire Lake Erie campaign. Perry, while a hero, never went on to greater glory and died at a young age from an infectious disease.

In the weeks that followed the battle, the British were forced to burn Fort Maulden and the Navy Yard before retreating up the Ontario Peninsula. William Henry Harrison and his army gave chase before being stopped at the Battle Of Chatham. But now, King George III was forced to deal with the fact that there were American soldiers occupying parts of Ontario and the United States Navy controlled the upper Great Lakes. It was the turning point in the War of 1812 and eventually forced the British to the bargaining table to end the conflict. And it all happened right here, in the Great Lakes, just 200 years ago...

The Battle Of Chatham

There is no doubt that Amherstburg, Ontario has played a great role in the history of the entire Great Lakes Region. It's true. This small piece of land, located at the mouth of the Detroit River where it meets Lake Erie's Canadian shore, directly changed our maps, our politics and our nationalities. What happened in Amherstburg also changed the lives of a King, a Chief and a U.S. President. It's quite a story, so you might want to gather the younger ones together and read this one aloud. I'll do my best to hold their interest.

From the very beginning of recorded history, the Great Lakes have been the grand prize everyone wanted to control. To the Native Americans, this was the richest hunting and fishing grounds in existence. When the Europeans came, they saw it as the source of great natural resources from food, to lumber, to furs, to semi-precious metals and valuable ores. As a young American Nation was born, it was seen as part of a great foundation to help build a powerful and independent country. Even today, we fight over the resources of these lakes, both natural and economic.

Before the American Revolution, when the British were the supreme power in the Lakes, they controlled the traffic between the upper and lower regions from their stronghold at Fort Wayne in Detroit. The river is narrow there, the land is flat, and the control was good.

But the Jay Treaty of 1799 gave Detroit and the fort to the Americans. To retain their position of regional power, the British crossed over to the Canadian side and moved downriver to a point where the river flowed into Lake Erie. Here, the visibility wasn't as good, but the river was even narrower. In fact, a medium sized garrison with a few ships could control the entire river from right here. And he who controlled the river, controlled the lakes!

This selected tract of land eventually became known as Amherstburg, home to Fort Malden and the King's Navy Yard. For several years, things went as planned: It was the British who controlled the traffic on the Great Lakes and the bounty of this rich resource went home to England's King George III.

There were many reasons on both sides for the War of 1812, as the Americans called it. Among them were the British disregard for America's rights as a nation of the world (The U.S. Congress was most agitated by the British Navy's practice of stopping American ships on the high seas and searching them for suspected British Navy deserters). The British and their Canadian colonists were still angered over American disregard for the property rights of British Loyalists after the American Revolution. Yes, there were definitely grounds for mistrust and ruffled feathers on both sides.

But when war broke out in the summer of 1812, Amherstburg found itself on the front lines. The British launched several successful invasions and campaigns in the Great Lakes theater of war from their base here. This was dividing the limited American forces between the Great Lakes and the East Coast and hampering American strategy. Frankly, the British were winning the war.

But then, in September of 1813, Commodore Perry defeated the British in the Battle of Lake Erie and Captain Barclay was forced to surrender the entire British fleet. Now, the tables were turned. With the fleet gone, the garrison at Amherstburg was now in danger. The American General, William Henry Harrison, had an entire army just across the river that outnumbered the British by a significant amount even when you counted the contingent of Indian warriors fighting for the British under the command of the Shawnee Chief, Tecumseh. The decision was made to abandon the fort and burn both the fort and the Navy Yard, before retreating up the Ontario Peninsula.

As the British retreated, along with them went Tecumseh and his contingent of warriors. It was early October by now. It was cold, rainy, and the British were under-supplied and low on morale. Tecumseh wanted no part of retreat, he wanted to make a stand and fight William Henry Harrison for personal reasons.

To make a long story short, Chief Tecumseh was originally from the Indiana Territory. He had tried to form a defensive confederacy of the Shawnee tribes in the territory to halt the western settlement of the White Man. In separate but questionable events, the then governor of the territory had cheated the Shawnee people out of a great deal of their land. When Tecumseh tried to raise a war party to retake the land, the governor led troops against the Shawnee stronghold at Tipicanoe and in Tecumseh's absence, killed the chief's family including his brother, who was the High Shaman of the tribe. Tecumseh had no choice but to flee to British-controlled Fort Malden with the remains of his great Indian Army and that's where he was when the War Of 1812 broke out. That governor, so hated by Tecumseh, was none other than William Henry Harrison.

As Tecumseh retreated with the British, he knew it was William Henry Harrison himself leading the American troops, and Harrison knew it was Tecumseh that led the Indian contingent.

Finally, the British made a stand along the marshy banks of the Thames River near what is now Chatham, Ontario. They were tired, cold and very hungry, not having eaten in two days. As the Americans advanced, the British fired one volley, then broke ranks and ran up the road towards Moravian Town. All that is, except the Indian contingent, now outnumbered four-to-one.

Harrison knew he was directly facing Tecumseh and he wanted nothing more than to "finish the job" he'd started in Indiana. Tecumseh knew he was facing Harrison and would not consider retreat in any form. The battle raged on for well over an hour, Tecumseh and his braves stopping the American advance cold in its tracks. Near the end of the second hour, Tecumseh himself fell, mortally wounded. Without their leader, the Indian warriors slowly retreated into the marshland and were gone. But the Americans had suffered heavy casualties and continuing their advance against the retreating British was out of the question.

The British re-grouped at Moravian Town and reinforcements arrived. What had been a complete route was turned around and in the weeks that followed, the British not only held their position on the Peninsula but in time, would drive the Americans back across the river. Tecumseh's stand is credited with not only stopping the American advance, but buying precious time for the British to re-group. Some say, his action prevented the entire Ontario Peninsula from becoming a U.S. state.

But because of the events of the summer and fall of 1813, the British high command had to rethink their strategy. They had been winning the war in the east, but now, in the Great Lakes, there were Americans occupying Canadian soil and their strangle hold on the lakes was gone. They desperately tried to secure control of the Niagara River to control all shipping from that point, but the various battles back and forth across that rocky terrain were as a group, indecisive.

Within a year, the war was over. The King of England had to grant certain guarantees to the Americans and never again would they control the bounty of the Great Lakes as they had before. In response, the British Army Engineers began planning an overland, water route that would connect Lake Huron directly to Lake Ontario. A protected waterway, deep within their boundaries that they could readily defend. Today, we call that waterway the Trent-Severn.

Barclay's career was now over. When he would eventually reach England again, he would face court-martial charges for his handling of the entire Lake Erie campaign. Perry, while a hero, never went on to greater glory and died at a young age from an infectious disease.

Tecumseh was honored as a hero, but he was one of the last barriers that had contained the western settlement of the American Pioneers. William Henry Harrison capitalized on his war record and his victory over Tecumseh, and was later elected President of the

United States. So much history, so many lives, all hinged around a small piece of land where the Detroit River meets Lake Erie…

Napoleon Takes Bobcaygeon...

The Boyd Family, for many years, was one of the most important and influential families in the Bobcaygeon, Ontario area. They owned a mill, land, and even livestock right there in the heart of the Trent-Severn Waterway. In fact, old Mossom Boyd himself not only raised prized, Double Standard Polled Herefords for the area's successful dairy industry, but in the late 1800s, he participated in a little experiment known as 'Cattalo,' or 'Beefalo.'

This was a cross-breeding of cattle for their milk, beef and meat products, and North American Bison, or Buffalo, for their heartiness and suitability to the harsh winters of Canada. Sounds like a great idea, doesn't it? Don't know if I'd want to meet one in a dark alley or even have my picture taken with one, but at the grocery store or the barbecue grill, it makes sense: plentiful milk and tasty beef at an affordable price because more of the animals survive in a marginal climate. Brilliant!

A great Bison Bull was acquired, named Napoleon Bonaparte, and put to work in the pastures. Things went well. It seems the cows all found Napoleon to be a dashing and likable fellow. And the calves worked out well too... until they reached about the age of three, when the wild buffalo genes would take over and the herd would become 'most unmanageable.'

Extra precautions were taken to secure these hybrid animals, being far bigger, more powerful and less docile than your standard, run-of-the-mill cows. At one point, the Boyds even resorted to putting the herd out on the 'big island' in Pigeon Lake. Thinking them safely off shore, they let them roam and graze in the summertime.

Unfortunately, Mossom Boyd underestimated two things: How lonely the herd would get way out there, and what truly wonderful swimmers buffalo can be. On one summer day around the turn-of-the-century, the herd of beefalo launched a surprise invasion of Bobcaygeon of the scale said to later influence the likes of Eisenhower himself.

When the bulls average about a ton each and the cows slightly less, cattalo can go pretty much where ever they want to. They were in the main street, they were in the shops and they were in the parks. And again, they 'went' where ever they wanted to!

The Boyds covered the damage to the town and eventually, the great cross breeding experiment came to an end. Once again, around Bobcaygeon, cattle looked like cattle and buffalo were hard to find. If you doubt that any part of this story may not be true, I offer to you, this piece of physical evidence: The head of the prize bull, Napoleon Bonaparte, was mounted and hung on the wall of the headquarters of the Boyd Lumber Company. That building is now part of the Boyd Heritage Museum and also serves as the Bobcaygeon Chamber Of Commerce Offices and Library. While the ownership has changed, certain aspects of the decor have not... Napoleon is still there, to this day!

Sackets Harbor, The History

Sackets Harbor is a small community near the far eastern end of Lake Ontario. Today, its principal industry is tourism, but the reason it's here, it's whole reason for being centers around the old U.S. Naval Base that once served this section of the Lakes. Sackets Harbor guarded the 'backdoor' into the very heart of our young country then and several incidents of historical note happened here. Perhaps the most important incidents are the two major battles fought with the British during the War of 1812. (You can read about those a little later in this same book!) Today, much of that battlefield has been preserved and is popular with summer visitors.

Near the eastern end of the battlefield, is the entrance to Navy Point where some of the most powerful ships to sail the Great Lakes in time of war were built. After the second battle for the harbor, both American and British efforts concentrated on ship building as a means to control the lake. Each ship built by each side was bigger and more powerful than the one before and with each ship launched, the balance of power on Lake Ontario would change.

One such example is the story of the *Superior.* Please be certain to read the story of "The Cable" later in this book. But perhaps the most famous ship built here never saw the water. The *New Orleans* was under construction when the war came to an end and could not be immediately completed due to the terms of the treaty that ended the war. They built a huge boathouse to protect their investment over the partially finished ship and moth-balled others in the harbor. The *Jefferson,* sank in her slip due to neglect and was claimed by the soft mud on the bottom of the harbor. Today, she is an active archeological dive site with many relics having been brought to the surface and put on public display. But the *New Orleans* didn't fare so well. She stayed in her giant boathouse until 1880 when the boathouse collapsed in a severe storm.

The *New Orleans* was now aged, represented outdated technology and was an eyesore. The Navy auctioned off everything they could with much of the wood being claimed locally and converted into home furnishings and structures in the town. If you are staying at one of the more historic B&Bs in the village, perhaps your host can point out a staircase or picture frame that was once a part of the gigantic, *New Orleans*...

You know, that's only the west-end history. The east-end history is even better! Out there at the edge of the village is a section of town referred to as The Madison Barracks. This is perhaps one of the most unusual historical communities I have ever seen. It began strictly as the name implies, an army barracks. But over the course of the years following the War Of 1812, the facility grew. Improvements and additions increased the size and scope of this facility many times as the importance of this outpost changed over the years. Some very famous names have called this place home.

In the 1880s, the 11th Infantry's band director lived here with his wife and young son. One day, the boy built a fort of stones on the Parade Ground and was instantly told by an officer to tear it down. The boy promised to do so and went home to get his wagon to remove the stones. But in his absence, another officer tore down the fort leaving just a pile of rubble. This enraged the boy and he immediately retaliated by throwing one of the stones through the offending officer's window. This would not be the last thing he would smash and break in his life. That boy was Fiorello LaGuardia, the future mayor of New York City who would win the hearts of his constituents by smashing illegal slot machines and gin barrels as part of his war on organized crime during the Great Depression. He is also well-remembered for reading the daily comic strips over the radio for the benefit of children whose families could not afford a newspaper in those tough times.

Another famous resident is credited with saving the Madison Barracks. In the mid-1870s, a fire ripped through the section known as the Old Stone Row and destroyed much of the facility. The Army considered abandoning the entire fort at that time. Had it not been for the lobbying efforts of an officer who served his very first tour of duty here and remembered the Madison Barracks fondly, they would have. But the officer had some political muscle. You see, by then, that young officer had risen to the rank of General... Grant to be exact, and at the time of the fire, he was also President of the United States. They rebuilt the barracks.

There is also a rather large cemetery in back of the long row of buildings where one more famous resident can still be found today. Major General Zebulon Pike was stationed here and beloved by his men. He was mortally wounded in the Battle of York (Toronto) and was returned here for formal military burial. A rather large monument marks the final resting place of this hero, who was also a well-known explorer of the great west before the war. In fact, a peak he discovered still bears his name today.

Today, Madison Barracks is a unique historic community in that many of the buildings are privately owned and serve as anything from restaurants, stores and shops, to apartment buildings and condominiums. Yes, there are a good number of buildings open to the public as museums too, but this unusual arrangement has many benefits and solved a major problem.

There were just too many buildings for the historical preservationists to restore and maintain. This was a big facility with much to save and preserve. The preservationists decided that rather than do a partial restoration on everything, they could do a complete restoration on the buildings they felt most important and save those for the public. By selling off the remainder, but controlling the nature of repairs and improvements as many historic communities do, they could use private funds to preserve the rest of the facility. And it has worked very well, thank you!

Madison Barracks is today, a joy to experience and see because of the preservationists and the private sector working together.

There are lots of reasons to put Sackets Harbor on your destination list. There are things to see and experience here you can find nowhere else. But letting me stand on that historical preservationist soap box I love so dearly, just one more time, let me tell you that you owe it to your past to visit here. This is where Americans long before us, carved out an existence and stood up to defend it in the face of the most powerful nation in the world. This was the back door that could have ended our experiment in freedom had the British tried their march from Horse Island just one more time. This, was America's very first outpost, built and established in the post-revolutionary period. It was the first outpost to be tested in time of war. And you know what? It's *still* there! Go see it!

The Battle Of Sackets Harbor, Round One

Yes, there were actually two battles for Sackets Harbor, New York, with one leading to the other and the other helping to lead to an uneasy end to the War of 1812. But let me put it all into perspective, and start with the beginning.

In 1801, Augustus Sacket bought the land that would soon become the town that bears his name. Here he found a beautiful, natural "snail shell" harbor with an abundance of natural resources close at hand. Among those resources were virgin forests with tall, straight trees "perfect for the fashioning of ship's spars." But there was another resource too, a political resource. Sackets Harbor was conveniently located on the southeast shore of Lake Ontario, very near to the St. Lawrence River and the Canadian border. The established businesses and industries of nearby Kingston, Ontario were hungry for all the timber and potash Augustus Sacket could send them. While he could make a handsome living selling his products just to American concerns, the Canadians would pay a much higher price and Augustus Sacket grew wealthy.

But there are problems in every perfect scenario. Relations between England and the United States were on a downhill spiral at the same time that Sacket was establishing his prosperous trade with the Canadians. Pressured by their war with Napoleon, the English Navy was known to stop American ships on the high seas, claim members of their crews to be deserters and press them into the service of the King against their will. This, along with other political ill feelings, lead to a series of trade embargoes with England and her possessions in the early years of the 19th century.

Those in the distant outpost of Sackets Harbor only saw the Federal Government as intruding on their trade bonanza and refused to comply with the restrictions. As the restrictions got tighter, the business concerns in Sackets Harbor resorted to out and out smuggling. Eventually, the *USS Oneida* under the command of Lieutenant M.T. Woolsey was sent in to "help the good people of Sackets Harbor enforce the embargoes." And that's where the *Oneida* was when war broke out in 1812.

On the morning of July 19th, 1812, the English ship *Royal George* was seen making way to Sackets Harbor with a very small flotilla. In reality, this was more of an exploratory voyage on behalf of the British and they were not prepared to invade the small settlement. But the Americans were convinced it would not only be the first battle of the war, but perhaps the most important.

The *Oneida* was positioned with one broadside of nine, 24-pounders facing the direction of the approaching ships. Her off-side cannons were removed from the ship and mounted on land, surrounding the town's only other defensive weapon, "Old Sow," an enormous, iron, 32-pounder. Remember, the weight mentioned refers to the weight of the cannon ball the gun fires, not the weight of the gun which was considerably more.

But there was a problem. The *Oneida*, only having 24-pounders on board, only had ammunition for their guns. "Old Sow" had none of the bigger rounds of her own. But they improvised and managed to wrap 24-pound cannon balls in carpeting sufficient to fire them from the larger cannon, but with decreased range and accuracy.

When the British came remotely within range, the Americans opened fire and startled their enemy who expected to find little resistance. The British returned fire with their own 32-pounders but being smaller, ship-mounted cannons, they lacked the range to effectively reach the American positions on the bluffs. After a long battle with little damage, one British 32-pounder did manage to hit solid ground, but only ground, behind the Sacket Mansion. And this is where the tide of battle changed.

An astute Sergeant realizing the value of that which had just buried itself in Augustus Sacket's back yard, immediately had it dug up and delivered to the cannoneers on the bluff. At last, a cannon ball that actually fit their gigantic "Old Sow!" They loaded it, took the most careful aim and literally "returned" the British fire. The cannon ball struck home and did significant damage to the *Royal George*. The British ships broke off the engagement and sped back to Kingston leaving both sides with new realizations and decisions to face.

First, the British now realized that the Americans were dead serious about this "silly little war." Second, the Americans were now convinced that the British desperately wanted Sackets Harbor and embarked on a program of building, fortifying and manning what would be the largest American military installation on the Great Lakes.

The Battle Of Sackets Harbor, Round Two

Less than a year after the first battle for the harbor, the second, and far more decisive battle took place. In the months that led up to May, 1813, the Americans had transformed the community into the largest military installation in the Lakes.

What had been a series of several smaller forts in the area, were linked together into one large fortification that nearly encircled the entire town. Out at the end of the peninsula that formed the snail-shell harbor, the Americans had also built one of the largest ship-building facilities ever known. And there were troops! Sackets Harbor had literally been invaded by a very large contingent of Army, Navy and Marine Corps personnel. If Sackets Harbor wasn't a target before, it certainly was now.

With their muscle and might, the Americans had already set about showing their mastery of Lake Ontario. They had already attacked Fort York (later called, Toronto), sacked both the city and the fort and plundered a great amount of supplies and equipment. In May of 1813, the fleet was off attacking Fort George at what is now Niagara-On-The-Lake when the British decided to retaliate. At the time, Sackets Harbor was defended by only 400 regular troops under the command of Lt. Colonel Backus who had explicit orders to summon General Brown over in Brownville to take command should the British make any advances.

On the morning of May 28th, 1813, Judge Kimball of Watertown saw a British fleet of six war ships towing scows filled with Red Coats through his spy glass on the horizon. He set off in the manner of Paul Revere to warn the surrounding villagers, but was ironically arrested for disturbing the peace and spent the entire battle in jail.

Fortunately, the watchman aboard the *Lady Of The Lake*, an American vessel known to be the fastest ship on the lakes, also spotted the British fleet. She tightened sail and easily outdistanced the British. She rounded Horse Island while firing warning shots from her only weapon, a nine-pound cannon on her bow.

The Americans leaped into action. General Brown was notified and took command while Lt. Colonel Backus sent out messengers into the countryside to call the militia to arms. Schools and shops were closed, church bells rang, farmers laid down their tools and every able-bodied man grabbed his weapon and ran to the defense of the harbor.

It was an awesome force the British had sent to face the Americans. Six British Battleships towing lines of flat-bottomed scows filled with British troops. But these weren't just any Red Coats, these were combat hardened veterans fresh from the war against Napoleon and ready to end this war with the Americans.

The British now recognized Sackets Harbor as a true military target if they didn't before. It was the base of all American operations in the area. It was also the "backdoor" to victory over the Americans. With the roads and canals now established from New York and Philadelphia to build up this installation, the British felt they could use these same routes to take the war to the most populated cities in the United States. Combined with their blockade of the coast, this could quickly end the conflict.

There were seven-hundred and fifty crack troops in those barges. Their intention was to land on the relative safety of Horse Island, which in those days, was connected to the mainland by a narrow, sandy isthmus. Since these were the days when the British preferred to wear red coats and march in straight lines, they could form their straight lines on the island, march across the sand and attack the fort.

But not all things go as planned. As the British were in view, but out of range... the wind died. And there those six battleships and seven-hundred and fifty crack troops in all those barges sat, bobbing on a becalmed Lake Ontario.

With this gift, General Brown had even more time to deploy his forces. He put out three rings of defense in front of the fort with the intent that as needed, one line could collapse into the next line closer to the gates of the fort. Eventually, if needed, they could make their last stand on the walls and parapets of the fort itself.

That first line of defense was a combined line of U.S. Army regulars and civilian militia holding positions behind overturned tables and other household furnishings donated by the citizens of Sackets Harbor. The second line was all militia and the third line, was comprised of Backus' combat-hardened Dragoons. All together, they were about eight-hundred in number.

Late in the afternoon, one of the British ships managed to maneuver itself within possible cannon range of the fort and launched a brief attack. But their cannon balls fell short and the attack was quickly ended. While it served no purpose to the British, it did to the Americans. Those cannon shots echoed through the hills and valleys of the surrounding countryside and those farmers and shopkeepers who had not heard the church bells *did* hear the cannons, grabbed their guns and started making their way to the harbor.

During the night, the British managed to land their forces on Horse Island and by morning, had sufficient time to organize their attack. At the same time, the American numbers had swelled to about one thousand with the addition of the late arriving militia.

On the morning of the 29th, the British started their march down the sandy isthmus and the Americans opened fire. For the next two hours, the British would march forward into the hail of American musket and cannon fire. Several times their advance faltered and they fell back to the safety of the woods on Horse Island, only to regroup and march on the fort again.

The lines of American defense were slowly caving in, one at a time. On the last advance, with the last of the Americans within the gates of the fort, a few red coats actually reached a small barracks building just outside the fort. This was their high water mark. With very limited cover and "no obtainable objective in sight," the British made a final retreat up the beach to the island and withdrew.

While the Americans had lost a scant, one hundred men, mostly civilian militia, the British had lost a full third of their entire force. They packed up their troops, loaded up their barges and departed for Kingston, leaving their dead and wounded behind. However, the most devastating loss to the Americans was at the Navy Yard. During the last British advance, a young officer had been misinformed that the battle had been lost. He then set fire to the yard and all its supplies to prevent them from falling into enemy hands. Most of these supplies were those captured at the Battle of York less than a month before.

In the months that followed, the war on Lake Ontario shifted to the mass building of bigger and bigger ships by both sides. With every ship that launched, the balance of power would change and the process would start all over again.

The Cable

In the times we have faced in recent years, I find it a good practice to look back on the actions of those Americans who came before us and the sacrifices they made for our country. I'm not talking about just the professional soldiers and sailors of our armed forces, though no one would question the roles they played. In this case, I'm talking about the average citizen, the men and women who lived in the towns and villages and enjoyed their new-found liberty in its earliest days. One of those historical events happened in the area of Henderson Harbor, New York on the southeastern shore of Lake Ontario. Now, more than ever, I feel it important to share that story.

In June, 1814, late in the War of 1812, things were not going well for the Americans. Even though Commodore Perry had handed a devastating defeat to the British in the Battle Of Lake Erie less than a year before, the British had retaliated with a stranglehold on Lake Ontario and the Niagara River. The American base at Sackets Harbor was as good as blockaded. The pressure was building and the stakes were the highest. If Sackets Harbor fell, Oswego would be next. Then, the canal routes inland, the back door to New York, Philadelphia and Washington, would be wide open for the British. This short experiment in freedom would be over and we would be forced to rejoin the English Colonial Empire. The threat was real, *very* real.

However, in the shipyards at Sackets Harbor, Commodore Chauncey had the *Superior*, what would be the biggest, baddest battleship on the lake when finished. She would change the balance of power on the lake and therefore, the course of the war itself. The hull was done, shipwrights were finishing her off and her spars were ready to raise. The only problem was that the heavy, rigging rope (commonly called "cable") was sitting on giant reels on the docks in Oswego… and the British controlled the lake!

As unlikely as it seemed to succeed, a plan was proposed. A rag-tag band of volunteers from both the Navy and the Marine Corps would unreel the cable, carry it on their shoulders and snake their way through the back roads all the way to Sackets Harbor.

The cable was moved by boat as far as Sandy Point, off-loaded and then the Sailors and the Marines took over. But the cable was heavy and the volunteers were few. Just outside the Village of Henderson, not that far from the harbor, the volunteers paused in exhaustion and the cable stopped moving. Word spread through the village that Chauncey's cable had stopped and that the volunteers were too exhausted to continue.

The Village of Henderson closed the shops and the schools. The church bells rang. Every able-bodied man, woman and child gathered on the road to Sackets Harbor and took their places in between the Sailors and the Marines. Together, they got that cable moving again. And as the cable moved through the farmlands on its way to Chauncey and the *Superior*, their numbers grew as farmers and their families put aside their labors and put their own shoulders to the cable.

So the bottom line here is, how much cable actually made it all the way to Sackets Harbor? It was enough to build a battleship! The *Superior* was launched, the balance of power shifted on Lake Ontario and within months, the war was over. The moral of the story is perfectly clear: Never, *ever*, underestimate the power of a people united!

Hi Ho, Trolley!

In the golden days of yesteryear, long before television, the trolley cars of Detroit were the principal means of public transportation. Their surface tracks and suspended electrical feed lines covered much of the city's main routes and could take the early 20th-century commuter pretty well wherever he needed to go.

This included routes all the way up Woodward Avenue through what is now the Cultural Center and right past the current School Center Building. But back in the early 1930s, this building was the home of WXYZ radio. It was in these studios, right along Woodward Avenue, that several famous radio shows of the era originated their regular broadcasts to the nation.

Sergeant Preston Of The Yukon, The Green Hornet and *The Lone Ranger* were among the most famous programs to call Detroit home. And as was the tradition in those days, they were broadcast live. In the specific case of The Lone Ranger, the broadcast itself was live, but the opening sound sequences which included the familiar orchestra pounding out "The William Tell Overture," Silver's thundering hoof beats and the announcer beckoning us back to those 'thrilling days of yesteryear,' were pre-recorded on a transcription disk and merely played back while the actors took their places around the microphone.

But times change, shows are eventually replaced and in the case of radio, it can even be supplanted by a more advanced medium. People forget. And then one day it can all come racing back from the past, and quite accidentally as in this incident told to me by my good friend, Jim Zinser.

In the late 1960s, the old studios of WXYZ now belonged to WDET and Wayne State University. Right next door was the transmitter site for WGPR television where Jim was then employed. During renovations to the WDET facilities, they came across a long forgotten closet containing some long forgotten articles from nearly forty years before. Among these items was a box of old transcription disks. Of course, the young engineers couldn't wait to hear what they had found and started plopping these records down on their modern turntables and pumping the audio through their state of the art sound systems.

Sure enough, up from one disk came the familiar strains of the William Tell Overture, the announcer's voice beckoning us back to the thrilling days of yesteryear, but there, right in with Silver's thundering hoof beats, were the distant sounds of bells!

It took the engineers some time to isolate and identify the sound, but finally, an older member of the staff who had grown up in the city recognized it as the distinctive bell of the Woodward Trolley. Apparently, the sound recording devices of the 1930s were far more sensitive and accurate than even the WXYZ engineers had known and obviously far more sensitive than the sound playback equipment of the day. These trolley bells had been riding right along with The Lone Ranger and Tonto, undetected for hundreds of broadcasts and had kept their secret for nearly forty years.

So the next time you hear the William Tell Overture, remember The Lone Ranger, Silver's thundering hoof beats, and the bells of the trolley you rode in Detroit last summer!

The Difference Between
The Army And The Navy

    The Trent-Severn Waterway is a series of lakes, rivers and canals, that connects Lake Huron's Georgian Bay, directly to Lake Ontario, bypassing entirely Lake Erie, the Detroit River and the Niagara River and Falls. The links in the waterway are a series of sophisticated locks that stretch across the Ontario Peninsula as the waterway rambles through some of Canada's most picturesque countryside dotted with quaint towns and villages. It's a wonderful trip! It's culturally rich and wonderfully historic. But wherever there are tales of great history, there are also tales of things some would like to forget… This is one of them.

    This tale was retold to me by a Parks Canada Naturalist and Historian who specializes in the Trent-Severn region. I have no reason to doubt him, but I have been unable to verify the story anywhere else. However, the opening of commerce and the timetable of the further development of the canal seem to support his tale. But substantiated or not, here's the story of the Bobcaygeon Lock.

    While it is celebrated that the first lock in the famed waterway opened here in 1833, it's a little known fact that the lock was not fully operational until 1835. There are always a few bugs to work out in a new system and this one certainly had a bug of Amazon proportions!

    Planning for the lock had taken years. The British Army wanted this system first as an American-proof way of moving troops and supplies deep into the Great Lakes system. The positions of the locks had been planned, and the first plans had been drawn. As the lumber industry began to flourish in the region, there also grew a commercial demand for the waterway. Finally, the go ahead was given, the money allocated and the British Army Corps Of Engineers went to work with the actual construction of the lock at Bobcaygeon.

    After great time and effort... it was done. And on that fateful day in 1833, the Army formed formations, the citizens crowded in crowds and officials made commemorative speeches. The lock was flooded and the very first boat entered from the high side. With a pull of the chains and the shifting of the gates, the water began to flow out of the lock and the boat rode the water down... to the bottom... literally.

With still some distance to go before the lower lock doors could be opened, there was a very noticeable 'thud' and suddenly the boat ceased to bob about. In fact, it started to list to one side and eventually it laid down on its side in water far too shallow to float. But of course, while the water was now low enough to open the lower doors, the boat was incapable of leaving the chamber.

How could this be? It seems that in the design of the lock, the Army Corps Of Engineers had failed to allow for the draft of the vessel! Perhaps it was an honest mistake. Perhaps it was a miscalculation of the changing water levels in the Kawartha Lakes in the days before computerized level control. Perhaps it was a misunderstanding of the nature of how boats work by someone with enough gold braid on his shoulders to not be challenged by subordinates. No matter what the reason, here stood a lot of important people looking at an expensive hole in the ground with a boat stuck in it. By 1835, the lock had been 'improved' and was fully operational.

The moral of the story: Never send the Army to do the Navy's job.

The Finger Of God...

(Note: This story originally ran as a sidebar in a feature article my magazine published on Lorain, Ohio. I am a fan of old buildings and architecture and while doing my research, I was disturbed that I kept running into historical roadblocks at the year, 1924. It was if nothing in town existed before that date. With a little more digging, I found out why...)

A tornado is nature's most violent storm. As residents of the Great Lakes, we are not strangers to their sudden attacks and swift destruction. Still, there is occasionally such a storm of such incredible strength, that creates such devastation, such loss, it reminds us all of our own fragility, mortality and puts our values into perspective. These storms are designated "F-5s" by professionals, the top of the force scale, the biggest a tornado can be... often called *The Finger Of God.*

Such a tornado struck Lorain in June, 1924. Nearly a hundred years later, it is still the most powerful such storm in Ohio history. That day, a young photographer named Rudy Moc and his friend, a newspaper reporter named Tex DeWeese survived the carnage and immediately set about recording the devastation in their combined words and pictures. A book was published entitled: *Lorain Tornado, Official Souvenir And Memorial Book.* Its nationwide distribution did much to fuel the relief funds and reconstruction efforts that literally brought Lorain back from the dead.

I have depended heavily on Mr. DeWeese's written, eyewitness account, along with several other sources, to bring you this recreation of events. If you would like to read all the text and see the photos, an existing copy of the above mentioned book is on file with the Black River Historical Society. I will warn you, Mr. Moc's photos clearly show the total destruction and devastation that leveled Lorain that evening, complete with automobiles wrapped around trees and entire blocks of brick buildings leveled to the ground. They *will* affect you. There are also other books about the disaster available from various online retailers. But this is what happened:

Saturday, June 28th, 1924 had been a hot and miserable summer day along the Ohio shoreline. The dark clouds and the muggy winds were enough to forewarn any Midwesterner that heavy weather was coming and in response, the Saturday afternoon shoppers hurried their errands so they could be home and dry before the impending storm hit. Escaping the heat were a good number of determined swimmers at Lakeview Park on the city's west end. Intermittent rain showers throughout the afternoon would chase them into the bathhouse, and once it had passed, they would venture back out onto the steamy beach. Another large group of people had opted to spend the afternoon and early evening in the State Theater on Broadway. Within these thick,
brick walls, they might not even hear the storm passing overhead… whenever it finally broke. Down the street, Tex DeWeese was in the Arcade Billiard Parlor.

By 5PM, Lorain was as dark as night and the rain came down in buckets. While Broadway itself was deserted, the street was lined with parked cars and the shops and restaurants were filled with last minute shoppers seeking refuge from the rain.

At 5:14PM, one of the most powerful funnel clouds in recorded history came in off Lake Erie at Lakeview Park. The bathhouse where the swimmers had taken refuge was first to go. It was torn from its foundation, killing several inside and injuring many more. The cars in the adjacent parking lot were either thrown down the bluff to the beach, or carried into downtown Lorain.

The residential section around 5th and 6th Streets was hit next. Homes and churches both were completely leveled. In the words of John McGarvey of the Black River Historical Society: "My Mother's house on 6th street was the only house standing on its foundation, though the roof was gone. Carpenters came and put a roof on that very evening so that everyone from the neighborhood would have a place to stay that night."

Lorain's main drag, Broadway, was hit the worst. As Tex DeWeese took shelter in the Arcade Billiard Parlor, he watched as an uncountable number of automobiles, horses and people, along with other unidentifiable debris, blew past the storefront.

In the State Theater, the roof began to give-way and the walls trembled. As panicked theatergoers dashed for the exits, the roof collapsed, bringing both levels of the balcony and part of the walls with it. Most of those who died in the storm, died here.

But the State Theater was not alone in its fate. We are accustomed to seeing pictures of wooden houses flattened by tornadoes. In severe cases, substantial structures such as commercial buildings and brick school buildings may be gutted by the high winds, but the walls are usually still there. The Lorain tornado ripped down Broadway literally tearing walls off brick storefronts and completely razing others.

The twister leaped over the Black River and plowed through the working class neighborhoods of the east end, devastating the shipyards that were also one of the community's financial mainstays.

And then, at 5:19PM, it left the Lorain city limits. Tex DeWeese refers to the storm as "only" five minutes in duration, but by the scientific standards of today, five minutes is a very long time for a storm of this magnitude to remain within an area the size of Lorain, Ohio. (1924 population was approximately 40,000.) It was obviously a slow-moving storm of incredible strength and much of the death and destruction it left behind can be credited to the time it spent working its way through the neighborhoods. The final totals were 78 killed, around 1,200 injured and financial damages estimated at $35,000,000.[00]. (That's in 1924 dollars!)

As soon as the storm had passed, Tex DeWeese crawled from the wreckage of the Arcade and began chronicling the event. Rudy Moc salvaged one of his cameras and began recording the carnage. The skies actually broke and the sun came out before sunset allowing the first rescue efforts to get underway.

There was no communication with the outside world. One young Ham Radio operator (not CB, 'Ham' as in Amateur Radio) somehow managed to string a wire antenna through what was left of the tree in his front yard and put his battery-operated transmitting set back on the air. His faint distress call was picked up by another Ham in nearby Cleveland who alerted the local authorities. Within minutes, a relief effort was launched that brought sadly needed medical supplies as well as doctors and nurses to Lorain yet that night… by tug boat, for the roads were all out. Once relief was on the way, these two Hams stayed on the air and brought the first reports of the disaster and the first messages from survivors to the outside world. (Think about their heroic efforts the next time your condo or home owners association wants to block this invaluable volunteer service from your community. Remember, on 9-11, the first service to go down were the cell phones. But the Ham Radio operators were there on that day, too.)

A make-shift hospital and morgue were set up at what was left of Central High School and the National Guard and Red Cross were summoned. When Henry Baker, national director of Red Cross relief out of Washington, D.C. arrived in Lorain, he declared "It is the most complete in devastation I have ever seen."

So, as you visit Lorain and spend a few hours in Lakeview Park, try to imagine that day in 1924 when the giant funnel came ashore, right here. When you walk past the historic buildings on Broadway, notice how many were built after 1924, and pay special attention to those that survived that day. And then pay close attention to the sky for while this may be the worst tornado in Ohio history, records are bound to be broken, someday…

The Ghosts Of Fort George

Fort George is a very old place. Originally built to protect the shoreline where the Niagara River finds Lake Ontario, it is now one of the most colorful attractions when you visit the village of Niagara-On-The-Lake on the Canadian side. It's a place shrouded in history, violence, war and the harsh life of the old frontier. Many lives have passed though these gates, and some even ended here. As time has passed, it has become more and more evident that some of those who perished within... have never left these gates.

Modern stories about the haunting began years ago when the fort was in reconstruction during the 1930s. There were the reported sightings of men in British military uniform walking across the grounds, the occasional sighting of a washerwoman near the entrance and the repeated sightings of a little girl wandering though some of the buildings.

Now that the fort is open to the public and staffed with costumed interpreters, telling the living from the dead has become more and more difficult. Frequently, visitors to the fort, in broad daylight, report trying to catch up with a uniformed guide who mysteriously disappears through a locked door or around a dead end corner. Mediums who have visited here often claim to have seen the spirit of a blonde-haired little girl who follows tour groups around the fort.

But it's at night that Fort George *really* comes to 'life.' Interest in the fort's haunted history and the persistent sightings of ghosts gave rise to one of the most unique tour opportunities you can experience anywhere in the Great Lakes: Ghost Tours of Fort George. They are run by The Friends Of Fort George and are conducted several times a week during the summer months, on Sunday nights only, in the fall, and then again, nearly every night of the week as Halloween approaches. Proceeds go to benefit this fine non-profit organization and you can find out more about schedules and ticket prices by contacting The Friends Of Fort George at 905-468-6621. But let me give you a taste of what you are in for...

We were in Niagara-On-The-Lake early one September to cover a story for my magazine. Near the top of our 'to do' list was taking the Ghost Tour of the fort so we could tell our readers all about it in time for Halloween. Imagine our disappointment to learn that after Labor Day, tours are Sunday nights only... And we would be long gone, by then.

But thanks to the efforts of the NOTL Chamber of Commerce and The Friends Of Fort George, we were put into direct contact with the man who conducts most of the ghost tours himself, and to our great surprise, he agreed to come to the fort on a Wednesday night, and conduct a ghost tour just for us!

By the time our guide, Kyle, arrived, it was later in the evening than most ghost tours. Chris was feeling tired and begged off a return trip to the fort, after all, we had been there all morning on the regular tour, and she was tired... Or so she said.

But this would be different, I knew. Even the brochure published by The Friends Of Fort George claim that the dead have come along on over 60% of these after-hour tours, "why don't you?" I rode with Kyle to the fort on a clear, calm night with a half moon. It's dark at the fort. There are no floodlights or streetlights in the immediate area. Kyle found the padlock and the great chain holding the fort doors closed, I think, mostly by feel. Just inside the doors is the Sentry Station and on the floor, in the back, is a small footlocker that holds Kyle's 'tools of the trade.'

It was so dark, Kyle couldn't see to work the combination lock on the footlocker without assistance. He finally forced the lock to surrender with the help of the light from my digital camera screen. Inside were the only things a 'ghost guide' needs at Fort George: a candle-powered lantern, and a long, flowing black robe that set the mood for a proper ghost hunt.

I was amazed at how much light that single candle within the glass lantern could produce, but seeing it was the only light in the fort, it probably made it seem brighter than it was. Without too much effort, I hung close to Kyle and the lantern.

"Over there," he said, "on that barrel outside the door to the cottage, often times we see the image of a woman. She sits on the barrel and watches the tour groups go by. We have no idea who she is or why she is trapped here. She makes no attempt to reach out to anyone on the tour and even fades away should anyone approach too close, but she watches us closely as we pass by."

I looked intently into the dancing shadows created by the trees and the faint moonlight. While I could see no woman on the barrel tonight, I had no reason to doubt this guide or the many people he had led through here on other moonlit nights.

Next, we passed by the first barracks building that today, holds large models and 3D map displays of the fort and the Niagara area. Earlier this day, Chris and I had stood inside that barracks as a costumed interpreter explained the layout of the fort and its relationship to the other military installations in the area at the time. It was truly a wonderful display… in the daytime. But now, after dark, it's thin, 'musket' windows and the misfit of the door around its frame were the only source of artificial light I could see anywhere.

"They leave the light on in that barracks at night as a security measure," Kyle said. "I really don't know why, but from the far side of the grounds, sometimes, you can see a British soldier pass in front of the window. Of course, by this time of night, all those who are *supposed* to be in costume have gone home..."

I can't tell you how unsettling it can be to be in a well-known haunted fort under these circumstances. Even though I am famous for bringing the 'ghost hunters curse' with me (when the ghost hunter's around, the ghosts leave town), I found myself growing quiet and feeling very unsettled. I had no idea this was just the start.

Next, we entered the long, second barracks... the big one. For the better part of the next half hour, Kyle stood in the solitary, flickering candlelight and proceeded to tell me stories of the many sightings that have occurred in this very room. The most noted is the recurring appearance of a small girl who claims to be Sarah Jean. She has shoulder-length blonde hair and a floor-length work dress inconsistent with the fashions and styles of the very early 1800s. She seems to have an attraction to Kyle personally and often appears on the stairwell leading to the second floor, and reaches out for Kyle's cape and hair during this part of the tour. Mediums have seen her as she follows the tour group out of this barracks and out onto the parade ground of the fort.

After repeated sightings of this little girl, local historians located the grave of a young girl about the same age with the very same name buried the churchyard in town. While her stone states she was the daughter of a British military family, her time on Earth was in the mid 1840s, not the earlier part of the century. However, that timeframe is consistent with her hairstyle and clothing. With a little more research, it was discovered that indeed, sections of Fort George were still in use during this period. So Sarah Jean isn't necessarily a figment of many people's imagination, she may simply be from a less famous time and less eventful place.

Other mysterious happenings in this barracks include the tugging of your clothing by unseen hands, the occasional push or shove by unseen persons and on rare occasion, the extinguishing of the Ghost Guide's candle for no apparent reason.

Back outside, Kyle led me past the Officer's Quarters and past the main cannon platform along the wall overlooking the Niagara River. Here he told me there has been the repeated sighting of a British Sentry walking along the elevated cannon platform forever keeping guard. However, he appears to be walking on his knees. More research revealed that when the fort was rebuilt in the 1930s, much of the landscape was 'leveled off' with construction equipment. With the Earth moved, some of the cannon platforms are not at the same elevation as they were in the original construction. It seems this Sentry is walking his post on the original planking, some eighteen inches below the reconstructed platform!

At this point in my tour, I began to feel quite edgy. I took several photos into the darkness, not knowing what would show up. Many of those photos I took by spinning around and shooting behind me hoping to catch someone off guard in the dark. But only the ghost hunter's curse was following me.

It was here that we reached the furthest point into the fort on the tour. Kyle and I stood next to the entrance to the Artificer's Building, on the path that leads down to the original Powder Magazine and the tunnel at the front entrance to the fort. He paused, or hesitated, really, and told me that this is the point, the exact spot where many of the tours turn back. People crossing the line past the side door to the Artificer's Building have been known to become physically ill for unknown reasons, and then to suddenly feel better once they re-crossed the line out of that sector of the fort. Others have complained of great feelings of sorrow on the same soil and some even weep uncontrollably. Some of the tour groups opt not to go down that path to the tunnel and on this night, my guide asked me in all confidence, if I would mind if we didn't go.

It was in that tunnel he saw his first ghosts in the fort: The shadow of a child that moved around the entrance to the tunnel, and then was replaced by a dark, shadow-like column that blocked the tunnel entrance altogether. Kyle admitted that on this night in particular, he was feeling very edgy and apprehensive about proceeding any further. Let's see. I was completely alone in a dark, haunted fort, with an experienced guide, and he says, *he's* getting too scared to go any further.

We turned back, but not before pausing for what seemed an insufferably long time in front of the Officer's Quarters. There Kyle set his lantern down on the ground and told me about the lady in the mirror. The mirror in the parlor room of the officer's quarters is an original furnishing in the building. On several occasions, daytime visitors to the fort have reported seeing a woman reflected in the mirror as she stands on the far side of the room. They turn, expecting to find a costumed interpreter ready to tell them about life as a

British Officer, but find no one there. More startling, during children's programs in the building, groups of young people have said 'how cool' the lady in the old-time dress was that came out and talked to them while their program director was getting supplies! They had no idea.

At this point, I was most unsettled and found myself watching the Officer's windows, the barracks windows, the cannon platform, and the parade grounds all around me. I shot several pictures of blank darkness in flash and in time exposure, both hoping to catch something on the disk, and to scare away whatever I may have caught. Then Kyle stopped midstream in his story and grabbed his lantern. He moved slowly from side to side trying to shift shadows.

"For a brief instant," he said, "I thought I saw someone next to the far barracks."

Probably the Provincial Police, I thought, wondering about all the flashing lights in the fort this late at night, or at least I was hoping it was only that. But whatever Kyle saw, was gone, and with a little encouragement on my behalf, we were too, very shortly thereafter.

After chaining and padlocking the door, and making our way to the Ravelin that protects the entry, we did have a genuine close encounter. Kyle stopped dead in his tracks and held out his arm to prevent me from another step. There in the darkness, his sharp eye had detected a very large skunk poking through the grass in front of the Ravelin. Our presence had set it on guard, but our sudden stop gave it an opportunity to slip off into the darkness with its scent glands still intact.

After our hearts started again, Kyle drove me back to the Angel Inn's Cottages where we were staying. I was exhausted, and honestly, glad the tour was over. This is one of those things you are compelled to do and once you've done it, you may not wish to go back. But you will always be glad you did, and it will be an experience you will never forget.

The Search For Swayze

Niagara-On-The-Lake, Ontario, is said to be the most haunted town in North America. Of course there are the several ghosts known to frequent Fort George, but there is also the old woman often seen in the rocking chair in the parlor of the Prince Of Wales Hotel. Those that can't see her, *do* see the chair move on its own. Then there are the two women whose voices can be heard arguing in one particular room of the Pillar And Post Inn. No one ever sees the women, but they can hear them and almost make out their muffled words. Occasionally, the maids enter that room to find the housekeeping work already done… to the best of the ghosts' abilities.

One more I need mention is the ghost of the cobbler who is still hard at work. Many of the buildings and cottages that line the business district were something else long before serving the community as they do today. One such cottage that provides overnight accommodations for those visiting the Shaw Festival was a cobbler's shop in the early 1800s. Occasionally, guests are awakened in the middle of the night by the tap, tap, tapping of hammer and nails. More than one guest has gone in search of the sound and entered the front room of the cottage to find the phosphorescent image of an old man bent over his cobbler's bench, hard at work. The ghost is reactive and seems as shocked to see the guest in his pajamas as the guest is to see the cobbler!

But without a doubt, the most famous ghost in all Niagara is that of Captain Colin Swayze of the Niagara Militia during the war of 1812. He is the spirit in residence at the famed, Olde Angel Inn at the corner of Market and Regent Streets. Long recognized as the most haunted place in Upper Canada, the Angel Inn has a long and difficult history.

It was built sometime around 1789 (though no one knows for sure), and was originally known as the Harmonious Coach House. It is here that those that formed Canada's first government over 220 years ago, celebrated their accomplishment with food and spirits, General John Graves Simcoe himself, in attendance.

During the War of 1812, the Inn was frequented by British soldiers from nearby Fort George and no stranger to the place was a young Captain named Colin Swayze. It is rumored that Swayze had a romantic attachment for a young woman at the Inn, either an employee or more likely, the innkeeper's daughter. There is no documented evidence of this but it does seem to fit the circumstances that follow.

During May of 1813, a surprise attack by the American Army overran the fort and the entire town. The invaders captured young Captain Swayze at the Angel Inn, rather than at the fort with his troops. As the story goes, the Americans tortured Swayze in front of the fireplace that still stands in the pub section of the main floor. Then they took him to the basement where he was stood up against the wall underneath what is now the bar, and shot with the innkeeper's flintlock that hung from a beam near the fireplace.

Several months later, in December 1813, the combined British and Native forces mounted their own surprise attack and drove the Americans back across the river, and then some. But on their way out of town, the Americans burned many of the buildings leaving much of the population homeless and literally out in the cold. One of the heavily damaged buildings was the Angel Inn, but it was rebuilt at the end of the war using many of the original support beams and other materials.

Unexplained happenings are not uncommon in the Olde Angel Inn and have been going on for a very long time. The first sign of anything out of the usual occurred during the rebuilding and redecorating at the end of that war. The image of the flintlock that once hung on the beam near the fireplace, returned. Its unburned profile is still clearly visible today, in the pub. Innkeepers since have tried to stain it, sand it, paint it and in any way imaginable, erase the image of the gun, but it has always returned. About a century or so ago, the innkeeper at the time gave up, varnished the whole beam over and made the musket part of the permanent décor. Of course, the assumed reason for the image's return is that this is indeed the gun that killed Swayze.

Other unexplained phenomenon includes the 'ghost banquet' that has upon rare occasion, taken place in the main dining room back behind the pub room. Here, one night after closing, the bartender sat in the darkened pub awaiting his ride home when he suddenly heard loud voices from the back dining room. He jumped up to investigate but when he hit the light switch, all sound stopped.

He returned to his seat near the front door only to have the sounds repeat, and again, they stopped as he entered the room. By now, his wife had arrived to pick him up, as she held a similar job in a pub across town and they often rode to work together. As she entered the pub, the sounds commenced again, this time, louder and more clearly than before. Along with it was the sound of laughter, moving furniture and breaking glass, it sounded like one wild party taking place back there.

When the couple reached the room and turned on the lights, they were shocked to see the room in a shambles. The tables were all moved and the place settings on the tables were all in disarray. Several of the glasses lay broken on the floor. While his wife began picking up the mess, the bartender searched the inn and checked all the locks. No one was found, no door or window was found open or unlocked and the door to the guest rooms upstairs was still locked. No one was there and there was no way anyone could have entered or left.

Upon leaving the Angel Inn, the wife noticed the British flag that hangs over the door was missing. Legend has it that as long as the Union Jack flies over the door, ghostly happenings are kept to a minimum. Occasionally, an out of town reveler has been known to take a souvenir and then anything seems to happen.

Another unusual experience guests have mentioned is the nocturnal visit by the Inn's resident cat. It seems that late at night, the cat seeks out the guests that are indeed cat lovers, and has been known to curl up on the foot of the bed, leaving sometime before morning. When guests have mentioned having the cat in their room, they are shocked to find out that there is no cat in residence at the Angel Inn, not a live one, anyway.

But that leaves us to discuss Captain Swayze himself. As I mentioned above, as long as the Union Jack flies over the door of the Angel Inn, Swayze seems to be content to stay on the main floor or in the basement. He has been seen, many times, scaring the bejeebers out of an unsuspecting barmaid sent to the basement to get more supplies (today, the room directly below the bar is used for kegs and storage of common bar supplies). They open the door to what is now called Swayze's Cellar, turn the corner and are shocked by the phosphorescent image of a man standing erect against the back wall. Once the bar maid vocally expresses her surprise (re: screams bloody murder), the spell is broken and Swayze literally fades away. Some years back, my wife and I were friends with then innkeepers, Peter and Diane Ling who shared their own story with me. Peter took over the Angel Inn a dozen years before as his 'retirement' from his corporate career in Toronto.

That first winter, Peter closed the Inn completely for some long overdue renovations and on many nights, he stayed there alone in one of the guest rooms. He will never forget the morning after he had granted an interview to a reporter from the local paper. In the interview, he was asked about the ghost to which Peter flippantly replied that he 'looked forward to being introduced to Captain Swayze but had not met him yet.' The very next morning, Peter was awakened by a loud pounding at the front door. When he got downstairs, he was amazed to see the Inn's 'lucky horseshoe' on the floor in front of the door. What was especially interesting was that this horseshoe usually hangs over the bar, *around the corner* from the entry. Add to this the multiple fresh dents in the wood that perfectly fit the horseshoe and Peter was wide-awake! He opened the door to see the latest edition of the morning paper on the stoop, this one bearing the headline: 'New Innkeeper Wants To Meet The Ghost.' Peter considered himself introduced and never challenged Swayze or his existence again.

Swayze has also been known to express his discontent with the wait staff by shaking and rattling the carefully sorted silverware bins making extra work for those on duty. This happens without cause, warning or explanation in the middle of a busy evening in the pub. Suddenly the bins start to shake like there's an earthquake just at that end of the bar, silverware jumps from bin to bin and then it's over. Of course, this can do great things to quiet a noisy pub and oddly, as soon as it stops, it does wonderful things for the sale of alcoholic beverages as well. Is Swayze just trying to quiet an annoying crowd or is he frustrated that none of these barmaids can see him and take his order?

On nights that Swayze wanders the upstairs, guests have reported waking up in the middle of the night to find their windows wide open, even in mid January. Doorknobs turn and closet doors creak slowly open by unseen hands as footsteps are heard in the hallway. Swayze has never shown a sign of being a malevolent spirit. In fact, his antics are more along the lines of practical jokes or simple poltergeist activity. Over the centuries, many mediums have visited the Olde Angel Inn and while none have ever claimed to make direct contact with the young Captain himself (being a good military officer, perhaps he knows when to keep his mouth shut?), all have described the same presence and concur that there is indeed, something here.

Me, My Wife & That Darn Ghost!

It was shortly before Christmas and my wife and I had planned a winter weekend getaway across the border in Canada. We piled into the car and off we went, filled with the spirit of the season, for three days and two nights of Victorian shopping in picturesque Niagara-On-The-Lake, Ontario. The shopping was wonderful and the Falls are beautiful when trimmed in snow, but it was our overnight accommodations that are the center of this tale.

We had arranged to stay at the infamous, Olde Angel Inn on Regent Street in the heart of the old village. If you need to be reminded of what this place is infamous for, let's just say that the Angel Inn is reputed to be the most haunted place in Upper Canada. The primary spirit is that of Captain Swayze, a British officer who died here during the War Of 1812. Legend has it that as long as the British Union Jack flies visibly over the entrance to the Inn, the ghost stays confined to the main floor and basement. However, should the flag be removed, his spirit is supposedly free to roam the entire building searching for those (probably Americans) who are responsible.

We had a lovely room on the second floor. As you entered, there was the bed, and at the far end of the left wall, a door that led to our private bathroom. It was small, but directly on the bathroom's opposite wall was another door that led to our own private sitting room. They had given us a suite! The sitting room was long and narrow with a small television and a love seat. There was also another half-bath at the far end. The rooms were arranged so that a person lying in bed could look through both bathroom doors and see the TV screen on a small stand in the sitting room.

Next to the bed was a window that overlooked the Inn's Regent Street entrance and just outside our window, flew the famous Union Jack... floodlight and all. Rest assured, this flag would be flying and visible twenty-four hours a day!

This had all the makings of a most romantic retreat. I blush at confessing to you, but my wife had even bought me a special gift to wear in our room for this weekend and surprised me with it on our first night there. Relax, it was a pair of silk boxer shorts bearing the multiple images of Daffy Duck dressed as Santa Claus. (Thanks, Avon Lady!) Obviously a turn-on to my wife, I wore the shorts to bed. However, some things come back to haunt you... no excuses for the pun.

It was our second night there. At around 4AM, my wife awoke and decided to use the bathroom. Of course, in the process of crawling out of that four-poster bed, she woke me, too. She flipped the light switch for the bathroom, but nothing happened.

"Ooh," she said with some reservation, "The bulb's burned out!" Then she noticed the heating unit in the wall wasn't working and a quick glance out the window at the street below told her the rest of the story. "The power's out!"

"But I can see the lights on Queen Street," I mumbled.

"It just seems to be our street that's out..." she cautiously answered.

Now I was awake. I turned over and could see out the window myself. Our streetlights were out. Everyone else's were lit. I also noticed that the floodlight illuminating the Union Jack was dark... While it was still there, just how visible was it now?

"I have a candle and some matches in my bag," said she.

"Get them," said I.

"They're over in the sitting room... would you go get them?" The thought of stumbling around in the dark, in Upper Canada's most haunted Inn, in my Daffy pants, was, shall we say, less than appealing.

"Why me?" I asked. And, with a great swallow of suffragette pride, she stammered:

"Because... you're the man." And after all that talk of equal this for equal that, too! We eventually agreed to go together. We cautiously stepped into the pitch-dark bathroom, me leading the way and my wife, grasping my upper arm, dragging along behind.

I could not believe it was so dark. Then I realized that the door to the sitting room was also closed... all but about an inch.

"Who closed the door?" I whispered. I certainly didn't want to surprise anyone that might be on the other side!

"I did," said she. "I didn't want anyone peeking in." There was no point in discussing the probability of encountering a fifteen-foot-tall Peeping Tom on the Ontario Peninsula in early winter. I ever so cautiously reached out into the darkness and gave the old door a nudge. It slowly swung open as if it were a prop from some 40s thriller, complete with creaking hinges and all. Eventually, it bumped to a stop against the wall in the sitting room. The moonlight through the sitting room windows barely illuminated the outline of the furnishings and shed darn little light into the bathroom itself. It was then I became aware of how tight my wife's grasp on my arm had become.

"Did you do that?" she whispered in panicked tones.

I suddenly realized, in the darkness, she had not seen my other hand shove the door. To her, it appeared to have opened all on its own. I quickly thought of all the nights I had to run to the store because she had forgotten to get milk on her way home. I thought of all the walls I had painted, holes I had drilled, things I had hung, only to re-drill, re-arrange and repaint. I thought of the wonderful opportunity that had just been handed me and God, I wanted to tell her "No."

But I am a coward. I thought about the death grip she had on my arm and about how much I enjoyed having this arm attached to my body. I thought about how she would never speak to me again during the rest of my undoubtedly short life. Then I thought about how she would wake every other guest in the Inn, who would then pound-in our door and discover my crumpled remains on the bathroom floor, clad only in my Daffy pants. I turned to her to say

"Yes," and reassure her that it was not some ghostly hand that had opened the door, but somehow, out of my mouth came the words:

"No, did you?" Then things got interesting. She cut off all circulation in my arm. In the subdued light, I could see she was screaming, but no sounds came from her open mouth. She was running away, that is her feet were moving. She was really pickin' 'em up and puttin' 'em down but she was going nowhere... probably because she was still tied to the dock... my arm. I knew there was a pending explosion and in the face of pure terror (her face was pretty scary!), I chickened out.

"Oh, you mean the door? Yeah, I did *that!*" I need not tell you the details of the conversation that followed other than it will be a long time before I forget this. We scrambled for the candle and set it on the shelf in the bathroom. It made a perfect nightlight, not that anyone in our room was going to get any more sleep that night, but it did take the edge off the darkness. I'll admit that I positioned it so what light there was, did shine out the window at least in the general direction of that Union Jack.

Very oddly, just as the sky was starting to gray-up with the approaching sunrise, the power came back. The bathroom lit up bright (that was a start!), the heat kicked on and the floodlight on the Union Jack went back on vigil. Was it Ontario Hydro solving the problem, or was Swayze just done cruisin' for the night? I don't care. How scary can the ghost be when compared to the wrath of my wife?

The Siege of Fort Erie

There were a lot of reasons the United States and The British Empire went to war in 1812. Without a doubt, one of the underlying causes was the struggle for control of the Great Lakes region. The Northwest Territory, as it was then known, was a wealth of resources and riches. There were animal pelts, fish, lumber and fertile soil as well as minerals and metals. The Great Lakes themselves provided a natural, waterborne highway on which to take this bounty to the world's markets. It was everything a world-dominating empire needed to extend its influence. Unfortunately, it was also everything a young, emerging nation needed to ensure its future. Conflict was inevitable.

There were no connecting roads or highways in the region. At best, there were a handful of wilderness trails that were, for the most part, uncharted and in many cases, unsafe for those of European heritage. The lakes themselves became the highways and it followed, that "he who controlled the lakes, controlled the Northwest Territory." And that was the driving force behind the strategies employed by both sides in this theater during the course of the war.

Just like opposing Little League teams stacking hand-over-hand on the handle of a bat to decide who bats first, the control of the Great Lakes was decided by who had control, further and further down the waterway. It started in the Straits with British control of the fort on Mackinac Island, and with that, control over who and what could leave Lakes Michigan and (by portage) Superior. But then the Americans took control of Fort Wayne at Detroit and in response, the British built a large naval yard and fleet at Amherstberg, In September of 1813, Commodore Perry defeated the British in the Battle Of Lake Erie, taking control of the lake and forcing the British to burn Fort Malden, the Navy Yard and retreat up the Ontario Peninsula.

The next logical vantage point to control the traffic on the lakes was the Niagara River. But just one ride along the Niagara Parkway will tell you why the struggle continued and the war dragged on. The Niagara River, while scenically beautiful, is a general's nightmare. Sheer stone cliffs stand guard over narrow gorges filled with white water rapids and deadly whirlpools. Quite frankly, there are very few footholds for attacker or defender along its unforgiving length, yet this is where the two opposing armies decided to play *King On The Mountain.*

There had been bloody skirmishes and short-lived invasions back and forth across the river since the very beginning of the war. It was often difficult for even the generals to determine who was in control of the waterway on a day-to-day basis. But it reached a climax in the late summer of 1814 at the very gates of Fort Erie.

In early July of that year, the Americans stationed at Buffalo, crossed the river and took Fort Erie by surprise. The fort fell to the Americans easily, as it was defended only by militia forces since the British regulars had been pulled back to York (Toronto). Then, the American commanders pointed their forces north, towards the Falls and the Lake Ontario shoreline at the far end of the river, in a final attempt to control its entire length.

British forces under Lieutenant General Sir Gordon Drummond were dispatched from York to stop the American advance. On July 26th, in what became known as the Battle Of Lundy's Lane, the two sides struggled to a draw in one of the bloodiest battles of the entire war. It was said that sounds of cannon and musket fire completely drowned out the deafening roar of the nearby falls.

Fearing their supply lines might be cut, the Americans fell back after Lundy's Lane to Fort Erie. The intention was to actually cross the river and take up a defensive position at the well-developed and properly maintained headquarters back in Buffalo, but several of the executive officers were severely wounded in the battle and Fort Erie became the holding ground out of necessity.

Drummond laid siege to the fort and pounded it regularly with cannon and mortar fire. Throughout August and into September the bloody standoff continued. At one point, the British captured one of the fort's bastions, but this victory was short-lived and ended with the explosion of the bastion's powder magazine. The British had suffered tremendous losses compared to the Americans.

The British pulled back into the woods and began the process of setting up a new line of siege guns grouped into three batteries. These new guns would probably spell the end of the American occupation of the fort if they were ever put into operation. The American commanders decided on a raid of the batteries before their completion and began to secretly clear a wide path through the surrounding woods in that direction.

Work was paced to keep ahead of the British construction and on September 16th, at 3:30PM, in the middle of a torrential downpour, sixteen-hundred American regulars burst out of the woods and completely surprised the British. They overran two of the three batteries and spiked the guns before they were stopped. Losses were heavy on both sides, but the British threat had been removed.

Discouraged, facing worsening elements and an army in declining health, Drummond abandoned the siege and simply marched away. Eventually, the Americans regrouped enough to withdraw to Buffalo and before the war's end, a British contingent did reoccupy the fort.

Today, the fort is restored and open to the public during the summer season. Costumed interpreters recreate life in the fort as it was during the American occupation and retell the story of the greatest siege of the War Of 1812. Not far from the very same bastions that were the prize for which so many struggled, a solemn monument quietly stands in memory of those who fell in the conflict.

Laura Secord, Heroine
And Chocolate Queen

Let me tell you about one of the most heroic and best remembered women of the Great Lakes Region: Laura Secord. She was a poor, simple farm woman living along the Niagara River during the War of 1812. But as history often does, it puts ordinary people into extraordinary circumstances. Such was the case one cold and rainy night when Laura Secord found herself running barefoot through the woods. She was on her way to the Army's Garrison Headquarters, miles away, to warn them of an impending enemy invasion across the river. Cut, cold and exhausted, she made it, and it was her advanced warning that changed the tide of the battle and for that day, the course of history.

Now, let me tell you about Frank O'Connor, the son of Irish immigrants. He was born in 1885 in Deseronto, near the far eastern end of Lake Ontario. In 1913, at the age of 28, he moved to Toronto with his young wife and opened, of all things, a candy store. But this was no ordinary candy store. The candy was made fresh right there in the shop, daily. It caught on fast. Soon, Frank was opening candy stores all over the city, and then all over Ontario… and then across Canada! But you never hear of O'Connor candies because Frank's wife thought she had a better name for the business: The Laura Secord Candy Company. There was something about the name that said, good, pure, and farm-fresh to Mrs. O'Connor and of course, everyone back then remembered the namesake's heroic deed. To this day, Laura Secord is a well-known brand name of candies in Canada.

But let me throw one last surprise at you here. We Americans have been enjoying Frank's wonderful candies for almost as long as the Canadians have. But you've never had a Laura Secord Chocolate? Well, when time came to open an American store to sell the candies, Frank faced a real dilemma. You see, Laura Secord was a well-known *Canadian* heroine. Her historic run through the woods that cold and rainy night, was to warn the *British* Army of an impending invasion by those upstart Americans. She was a British Loyalist! Frank feared the name of the brave woman whose efforts ensured a significant British victory, was not the best marketing tool to help sell his candies to the Americans. So, for the chain of stores on the American side of the border, Laura Secord changed her name to... Fanny Farmer.

The Legend Of
The Maid Of The Mist

As the story goes, many generations ago, long before the White Man came to Niagara, the Native People lived here in peace under the protection of spirits known as The Thunder People. The Thunder People are said to have lived in a series of caves behind the great falls and spoke often with the human beings of the land of Niagara.

Before humans lost the ability to speak with the wind and the sun and the earth, the Thunder People would share their knowledge with the Humans and they told them everything they needed to know to survive Niagara's harsh climate. Back then, young braves would test and prove themselves by paddling birch bark canoes over the falls. but the Thunder People would catch them, and gently set their canoe in safer water and tell them, "they didn't need to test themselves in this way,"

The last human being who spoke with the Thunder People was a young Indian Maid. When she was but a girl, she had fallen asleep under a tree near the falls. While she slept, an evil spirit that resembled a snake crept up on her and hid within her clothing. When the time came for the young maid to marry, the marriage produced no children and soon, her husband died, Eventually, she remarried and again, there were no children and all too soon, the husband died.

After the loss of a third husband, the Maid became despondent and one day, took off in a canoe near the top of the falls and paddled towards the mist and the certain death that awaited her in the powerful cataract. But the Thunder People pulled her from the water and brought her to their cave behind the falls. As she dried out, they made her stand above the fire, completely covered in the smoky plume. Soon, the evil spirit that looked like a snake could take no more and left her body, slithering off down into the darkness of the cave.

The Maid was put back in her canoe and sent back out through the mist at the bottom of the falls to return to her people. She married one more time and this time, produced a large family and lived a long and happy life with her husband. But no one heard the voice of the Thunder People ever again. Some tribal elders felt that human beings just lost the ability to hear them, others feared the Thunder People had become angry and moved away. Their empty caves were soon discovered. Yet some felt they were driven out by fear of discovery as the White Man began to explore the area.

For whatever reason, the last human to hear the Thunder People, the last human to be spared the vengeance of the great falls, the last human to make the return trip through the mist by the grace of the Thunder People, was the Maid Of The Mist…

The One, The Only, The Great Farini

In a non-descript grave in a quiet church yard in downtown Port Hope, Ontario… amongst all the Smiths, Coopers, Wrights and other recognizable names of the community's strong English heritage… there, in the middle of all that, is buried Port Hope's most famous resident. The headstone is marked: Antonio Guermo Farini, 'The Great Farini.'

So who was this Great Farini guy? He was *only* the most famous tightrope walker of all time! He was an aerial acrobat extraordinaire and in his day (the mid to late 1800s), he literally performed before all the crowned heads of Europe and millions of awe-struck admirers around the world. This is the man whose picture you have seen many times as he walked the tightrope across Niagara Falls. Once he did this with a washing machine tied to his back. On another occasion, he offered to carry the Prince of Wales across during the Prince's visit to Ontario. The Prince (Queen Victoria's son and a rather portly gentleman), declined. The Great Farini was the first to do many of the things circus goers expect today and he did them all with an unmistakable panache.

He was also an explorer, a painter, an author, an expert botanist, he spoke seven languages, and there is evidence he may have also served as a spy during the American Civil War. On top of that, he was also an inventor and the genius behind hundreds of innovations from folding theater seats to the modern parachute. So why is this innovative, daredevil named Farini, buried here, in the middle of this quiet British settlement? Well, he grew up here! But back then, everyone knew him better as 'Bill Hunt.'

William Leonard Hunt grew up on the family farm on the outskirts of Port Hope. One day in 1853, he went to town to see the arrival of the Barnum and Bailey Circus. Young Bill Hunt was mesmerized by what he saw, especially the tightrope walkers. He went home and stretched a similar rope across the hayloft in the family barn. For the next seven years, he practiced in secret until one day, he came to town and announced he would stretch a rope across the Ganaraska Rapids, from two of Port Hope's tallest buildings, and he would walk it!

A crowd showed up. They chanted, 'Don't do it, Bill!' But secretly, everyone waited with baited breath for the inevitable to happen. But it didn't. Bill Hunt stepped out on to the rope and walked high above the rapids. He did tricks, he stood on one foot, on his head. For an hour and a half, he mesmerized the crowd every bit as much as he had been mesmerized as a young boy.

That was a day that changed local history and launched the career of the most famous man to ever walk the high wire. It may have been Bill Hunt that went up the rope, but it was the Great Farini who came down.

The complete biography of William Leonard Hunt was written some time ago by a local author named Shane Peacock. His book, *The Great Farini*, is still available today on Amazon.com. After speaking with Shane myself, after seeing just a few of his rare pictures of this remarkable man, I'm sure you would enjoy his book a lot!

The Day Dave Bombed Detroit

During the time we published *Great Lakes Cruiser Magazine*, my wife and I were fortunate enough to spend several days onboard the *Kawartha Voyageur*, a cruise ship traveling Ontario's Trent-Severn Waterway. At the time, we were only in our early forties while most of the passengers on this trip were senior citizens. Most of them were older than our own parents! But I have to tell you, we enjoyed their company immensely. We met retired school teachers and corporate executives alike and heard some very fascinating and entertaining stories from them all.

One man in particular, Dave, shared a story with us over dinner one night that I will never forget. Dave celebrated his seventy-fifth birthday on board but during World War II, he was a young lad in the Royal Air Force. Dave taught Air Force navigation, specifically, he taught bomber squadron crews how to find their targets and how to get home again.

Very early in the war, Dave was transferred to an Ontario base near Lake Huron, as the skies were safer for instruction there. One day, the Americans, who had just entered the war, called and asked the boys of the R.A.F. if they would make a mock bombing run on Detroit so that they could practice scrambling their air defenses and anti-aircraft trainees. The R.A.F. was glad to oblige as it would make an excellent exercise for their own crews.

However, the R.A.F. boys had already been at war for two years and what would be expected, standard procedure to them, was not viewed the same by their inexperienced American counterparts. The R.A.F. planned a course that took them east from the Port Huron area, zigzagged across the Ontario peninsula, entered Lake Erie and then they made their attack run on Detroit from the south, southeast. To them, this was good logical practice and an exercise of standard difficulty.

Unfortunately, the Americans had expected the bombers to just come straight on down the St. Clair River and hit the city head on from the northeast. This meant that when the R.A.F. got to Detroit, they were very much alone. No one (of the military persuasion) had seen them coming. And worst of all, no one would see them go. There is no glory in a stunning victory if there are no witnesses and no way to leave your mark.

But necessity is the mother of invention and low and behold, each bomber carried on board a full, fresh-from-England-supply… of toilet paper. Now, for those of you who don't know, British toilet paper is not high on their list of popular exports and there is a reason for this. The toilet paper the R.A.F. boys could buy locally in Canada was much preferred, and very reasonable. However, the rules state that you must first use what the Crown provides… so they used it.

The bomb racks in all the planes were quickly stuffed with every last roll of British toilet paper that could be found. The planes circled about and harmlessly dumped their load on unprotected Detroit. There was toilet paper everywhere! There were shocked citizens on the ground. There were angry American voices on every channel of the radio… but to this day, to my knowledge, this is the only time an entire American city has ever been T-Ped! Leave it to the rascals of the RAF.

The Art Of The Inn

Gore's Landing, on Rice Lake in the heart of Ontario's Trent-Severn Waterway, has always enjoyed a reputation as a place where artists and writers gather... a place of arts and letters, as it were. Well-known Canadian author, Catherine Parr Trail was no stranger to this shore and wrote some of her best works while living here and at Wolf Tower, just a mile or so west along the shore.

John David Kelley was born here in 1862. While his skill at painting historical scenes caused him to travel widely, this was his home. After his wife and infant son died in childbirth, he spent many of his days quietly working in a one-room studio along what is now called Kelley Road in the village.

There were many other artisans with strong creative ties to Gore's Landing including Rhoda Anne Page, Archibald Lampman (Lampman Street), Charles Fothergill, Frederick James Rowan, J.C. Braithwaite, and of course, the well-known water colorist, Reginald Drayton.

But of all those who explored their creativity in and around Gore's Landing, perhaps none is as famous as Gerald Sinclair Hayward. Hayward was born and raised in the Rice Lake area and spent much time in Gore's Landing. After attempting several other more conventional careers, he followed his talent into the painting of miniatures. By the turn-of-the-century, he was one of the most prominent and sought after portrait painters in the world.

He came back to Gore's Landing and built a lavish summer home on the lakeshore. There were magnificent wrap-around verandahs on both the first and second floors with a turret-room at the top of "the tower." It was definitely a "country home" with beamed ceilings and thought provoking alcoves. He named this residence, "The Willows" after the abundance of the tree by the same name on his property. He vacated The Willows in 1908 and rented it to a Cobourg businessman. However, he still came back to

Gore's Landing in the summer months up to his death in 1926 and is buried in the cemetery up the hill at St. George's Anglican Church. The Willows was eventually sold and then, became an inn... the Victoria Inn.

Hayward literally left his mark here. Not only did he donate large sums of money for the building of several churches (including St. George's) in town, he was also known to idly carve on whatever wood was about when the mood struck him. If you stroll over to the wooden beams to the left of the fireplace in what serves as the lobby of the Victoria Inn, you will find a decorative moose he carved into the supporting structure one evening well over one hundred years ago for reasons that have been long forgotten. Donald and Donna Cane, current owners of the Victoria Inn told me that there are a couple old picnic tables out back with similar carvings, and stained with whatever Hayward was having for lunch that day...

A visit to the Victoria Inn today is a rewarding experience whether you come for lunch, or the weekend. The dining room (what was once Hayward's verandah) is open to the public. The inn serves three full meals daily from a well-rounded menu and the food is first-class. The inn itself still enchants memories of its colorful past including delightfully un-even wooden floors, Victorian gardens and cedar shake exterior. The rooms are cozy, with fireplaces and private baths. On the second floor, the verandahs were also walled-in to accommodate individual plumbing for each guest room. As you shower, remember this used to be a porch!

Creativity and artistic expression are still very much alive in this house. A small entry room near the lobby was set aside as a small country store, selling the artwork and sculpture of local artisans. It met with such popularity with the visitors and guests that it kind of "spilled out" into the living room and dining room. Many of the paintings and light fixtures you see are indeed for sale. The lobby is brightly decorated with quilts, sculptures and cabinetry that is again, for sale. And next to the front counter, there is a large glass display case that holds other works of local art... and a cat! The cat is not for sale. In fact, two cats live here. Beware the three-legged cat, he loves wheat toast!

Outside, you will find the work of one more artist I simply must mention: Basil Dey, He's a retired GM welder with a flair for natural life. He has created, out of welded iron and left over machine parts, a complete menagerie of animals that grace the gardens of the inn. My wife's favorite was a small rooster complete with robust tail feathers. I rather liked the peacock, whose tail was comprised of brightly painted iron rods, welded together with machine washers giving it an amazingly life-like appearance. But his masterpiece had to be the lady on the bicycle... her body was an old milk can and her hat was once a street lamp shade.

Canada's Favorite Son

Virtually unknown in the United States, are the works of Stephen Leacock. I cannot tell you why, for his collective works are many, good, and most of all, very funny! Leacock (1869-1944) was Canada's most beloved humorist... not a comedian, but an author who had an eye for the obvious even when the rest of us did not. His works are inspired essays on the state of human kind and he captures the very essence of the Canadian heartland.

Perhaps that's why we in the states are so ignorant of his work. His favorite audience was his own countrymen with whom he shared a culture and a history. We had Mark Twain, they had Stephen Leacock. And in perspective and prominence, they both fulfilled similar roles in their own worlds. But I must confess, while Twain writes of young boys in a much earlier America, where high-tech devices were limited to steam boats and rafts, Leacock was a more modern man and much of his work speaks of life in more familiar terms to us all.

The very first time I heard a Stephen Leacock story was aboard the *Kawartha Voyageur,* the cruise ship that travels the Trent-Severn Waterway across the Ontario Peninsula. We were docked in Orillia for the evening when the Captain arranged for someone from the Leacock museum to come to the boat and read to us from the famed author's works. We all sat there mesmerized like school children for page after page of these delightful short stories about kids and old ladies with loud radios and more. What a treasure these people have in a man that could write such charming, tongue-in-cheek tales! Imagine my surprise when I found out he had been dead for over half a century. That's how timeless his work really is.

We didn't get a chance to visit the Leacock museum that trip and it was our loss. Don't make it yours. This 'museum' was Leacock's summer home, a beautiful mansion he built in 1928 on nine-and-a-half-acres of rolling greens on the shores of Lake

Couchiching in Orillia's east end. Actually, he bought the land in 1908 but the best things are worth waiting for. This home was an inspiration to him and he created his best works, right here.

In the museum are many manuscripts, artifacts and photographs celebrating the life of Stephen Leacock, but that makes it sound like a very 'stuffy' museum Mr. Leacock wouldn't have enjoyed himself. So they also opened up the home's tea room as the Wissanotti Terrace Cafe, and serve a wonderful lunch and High Tea. There is a full schedule of seasonal special events held in the museum and on the grounds. There is also The Children's Discovery Place exhibit in the boathouse at the shore. It's a hands-on interactive collection of exhibits that includes a tree house, costume and stage area, and a slew of puzzles that let young people and their parents discover and relate to Leacock in their own way. All this goes on, in the very rooms where the great author really preferred to write.

Stephen Leacock is a Canadian National Treasure that they are willing to share with us. Take your time in Orillia to discover this great talent and the environment that inspired him. This is a 'Don't Miss!'

The King Of Beaver Island

Of all the stories I have collected from around the Great Lakes, this one is perhaps the strangest of them all, bordering on the completely Bazaar. But... did you know that for a brief time in the mid-1800s, Lake Michigan's Beaver Island was considered a separate country and was actually ruled by a king? It's true! And the story of how this came to be, and how it all faded into history is quite a tale, indeed.

In 1844, the center of the Mormon religion was in Illinois. But in that fateful year, their leader, Joseph Smith was shot and killed in a mob riot over a closed printing press. As the church reformed, the vast majority of the Mormons followed Brigham Young west, to Utah, where they founded and settled Salt Lake City. That's pretty well known history and please, do not confuse these fine people in any way with those in this story. They are completely different organizations!

What many people *don't* know is that a small faction of that original group followed a different leader north, into Wisconsin and from there, out to Beaver Island, Michigan. The leader of the splinter group was James J. Strang and in 1847, he and a small number of his followers permanently settled on the island. While the frontier people who inhabited the island eyed these newcomers with suspicion due to their different religious beliefs, Strang himself saw Beaver Island as a tremendous opportunity.

Here, there was what seemed like an unending supply of timber to cut for cordwood to sell to passing steamers. The waters of northern Lake Michigan were filled with fish to the point where even inexperienced fishermen could earn a good living. Even more important, there was isolation from the rest of Christian society as well as the rest of the Mormon Church that questioned and challenged Strang's authority as a leader. Over time and with many trips back east, Strang won more and more converts to his way of thinking and brought them to the 'promised land' of Beaver Island. In short order, despite the best efforts of those who opposed the Mormon migration, Strang's following became the voting majority on Beaver Island and he now became a political force.

Back then, Beaver Island was part of Mackinac County with the county seat and government on Mackinac Island. At that level of government, he still faced much opposition, not just because of the religious issues, but due to his business practices. Strang and his followers were aggressively taking over and challenging the Christians in every phase of life from fishing grounds to public position and employment.

Local ordinances were passed that allowed Strang to confiscate fishing boats and nets owned by non-Mormons who strayed into 'his' waters. Public positions such as Sheriffs, lighthouse keepers and postmasters were now filled by Mormons who tailored their efforts to best serve Strang and his followers. Accusations were made of dark-handed dealings that even included thievery and piracy! One particular charge centered around the Mormon lighthouse keeper at nearby Skillagalee dowsing his light, and even flying false lights on dark nights when Christian cargo ships would make their way up the lake. When the ship would eventually wreck on the treacherous reefs in the area, Mormon crews would 'salvage' the hulks for anything of value and on several occasions, they were accused of murdering the survivors.

However, with a Mormon Sheriff in place, all such charges fell by the wayside. When those at the county seat on Mackinac Island protested too loudly, Strang got himself elected to the state house and successfully pushed through legislation that moved Beaver Island from Mackinac to Emmett County. And when tempers and protests rose again, Strang declared the Island free and independent of the United States and established himself as King of this small, new country.

By now, Strang's 'church' had taken on a cult-like atmosphere. But power does corrupt and Strang was now the ultimate power in northern Lake Michigan. He had forbid his followers to engage in polygamy, the practice of having more than one wife as many Mormons did in those days, declaring it an abomination against God. However, when his nephew and personal secretary, Charles J. Douglas, who traveled with him everywhere, gave birth to a baby boy... Strang was forced to reveal that 'Charles' was really Elvira Field and that he had taken her as a second wife. According to Strang, God secretly revealed to him that it would be alright for Strang to *personally* practice polygamy, because he could *afford* two wives. Soon, other prosperous men in the colony wanted the right to practice polygamy causing yet one more topic of contention between them and the Christians that surrounded them.

As there are in any cult-type following, there were those who had become disenchanted with Strang and had left the colony. Perhaps 'disenchanted' is not the correct word as several had actually joined forces with the Mackinac County opposition trying to force the Mormons from Beaver Island.

It all came to a head in late June of 1856. What one-hundred and fifty years of hind-sight might label as a 'plot' began with the arrival of the U.S. Battleship *Michigan* at St. James Harbor. Strang was summoned down to the dock on the official request of business with the captain when two of the colony's disaffected followers leapt out in surprise and repeatedly shot Strang in the back, mortally wounding him. (Strang would eventually die from these wounds some three weeks later, back at his parent's home in Wisconsin.) They even pistol whipped the fallen leader before running up the gangplank of the *Michigan* and asking the protection of the United States Government.

The captain granted their request and refused to surrender the two assassins to the Mormon Sherriff. Instead, they transported the pair back to Mackinac Island (even though the state now recognized it as a different county) and turned them over to authorities there.

They were 'arrested' and placed in an unlocked cell where the local citizenry called on them to offer congratulations. If the ladies weren't bringing them baked goods and home cooked meals, their men were taking them out for dinner and drinks at the Island's finest establishments. A 'trial' was held, but since no Mormons showed to testify and the only other witness, the captain of the *Michigan,* had long left port, all charges were dropped due to lack of evidence and the assassins were freed.

With Strang gone, an organized flotilla of vessels from the various shores of Mackinac County arrived within days of the shooting. There, they stripped the Mormons of virtually all worldly possessions and forcibly deported them from the island, setting them ashore to fend for themselves at various ports around the southern end of the lake.

Obviously, the government and administration of Beaver Island, once again part of Emmett County and the State of Michigan, changed overnight. And while the Mormons were gone, there are still traces, structures and a few named places that remain today, reminding us of King Strang and the Country of Beaver Island...

The Lakeshore Engine Works

Down near the waterfront in the lower harbor of Marquette, Michigan, sits an old warehouse that until recently, had seen better days. Once, many of the windows were boarded over, but now, fresh paint covers the walls, hiding ghosts of management and advertising long past. You can't help but walk right by this old dinosaur on your way from the marina to the Vierling House.

"What is it?" I asked our faithful scout. "Something that used to be a lot more interesting," came the answer. Right then and there, I knew, I had found a *story*!

It seems this old building was once the Lake Shore Engine Works and for a number of years in the days prior to 1900, they produced a one cylinder, gasoline marine engine that soon became the standard of the U.S. Lifesaving Service. Truly, mining machinery was the company's bread and butter, but this little marine engine would rapidly change the world as boaters would know it.

After several years of development, the "Superior Engine" as it was called, was first tested in 1899, in the local Lifesaving crew's surfboat. It performed so well, soon the company had orders to motorize the entire fleet. One of the engineers on this project was a Swedish immigrant named Nels Flodin.

As far as Nels was concerned, the idea of motorized travel on the lake was great. But the biggest drawback of the Superior Engine was that it was an inboard, permanently mounted to the hull of the boat. For someone like Nels, who loved to fish, this meant a very cost-prohibitive investment of buying a whole new boat. If only there was a way to make the unit lighter and more portable…

Being an engineer, he tinkered and designed in his spare time and by the summer of 1898, he had developed a prototype version of the Superior Engine that could be hung over the back transom of a standard boat. It was… an outboard motor! To Nels, this was a major convenience but to others watching him putter around on the waters of the lower harbor, it proved to be a major opportunity.

History goes dark here, if not by confusion, perhaps by design. The remaining history of the development of the outboard motor is shrouded in claim and counter-claim. A Detroit area patent attorney named Cameron Waterman was no stranger to the area and even had contacts at the area's prestigious, Huron Mountain Club where several of the Lake Shore executives were also members. Suddenly, Waterman took out patents on such a device and went into business building them in Detroit under the name of the Waterman Marine Motor Company. His first units were built by Glenn Curtis of aircraft fame and tested on the Detroit River in 1905. In later years, Waterman would claim "other devices" were not patented or were imperfectly patented. Remember, he was a lawyer, not an engineer. The Waterman Marine Motor Company is still around today in a more memorable incarnation as Mercury Marine. But the Waterman Company wasn't the only firm to spring from Flodin's fishing experiment. There was another engineer at Lake Shore, another Scandinavian immigrant who was friends with Flodin and probably even made a few suggestions to help get that first one on the water. His name was Ole Evinrude…

As an epilogue to this amazing story, I can tell you that Ole's Grandson, Tom, still lives in the Marquette area and is acquainted with our faithful scout. Also, I can tell you that the original Flodin engine is now among the missing! Quite some years ago, before we worried about preserving pieces of the cultural past, it disappeared. A noted local historian is convinced it hasn't gone far, and is merely "lost" in someone's garage or basement, abandoned behind the old fuel oil tank.

Albert Ocha,
Death Of A Hero

      The history of the United States Life Saving Service is filled with true stories of heroic men faced with impossible situations. It was within the ranks of this organization, a precursor to the modern U.S. Coast Guard, that the well-known adage was coined: "You have to go out, you don't have to come back." This referred to the dedication of the Surfmen in the service to venture out into the raging storms, in the black of night, in hopes of saving but one life. Truly, they were heroes all, but none represents the service and its dedication more than the legendary Albert Ocha.

      Albert Ocha grew up in Port Hope, Michigan, on the Lake Huron shore. In 1882, at the age of 18, he joined the Life Saving Service as a Surfman in what is now Tawas. His skill and courage brought him up through the ranks quickly and he was promoted to the rank of Keeper for the Portage, Michigan Station on Lake Superior at the tender age of 23.

      It was here, battling the greatest of the Great Lakes that Ocha earned much of his legendary reputation. On one occasion, the call went out that a ship had gone aground in a fierce winter gale near Marquette. The crew was stranded and would surely perish as the storm slowly beat the wreck to splinters. While everyone else admitted there was nothing to be done, Albert Ocha commandeered a train, loaded his entire crew and their surfboat onto a flat car and raced the one hundred and ten miles to the wreck site. There, they launched into the pounding surf, into the darkness, into the howling snow... and they saved the day! Once he proved the impossible could be done, he would do this several more times during his career. His exploits became legendary and he held the highest respect of his peers.

In the years that followed, Ocha married and started a family. In fact, he left the service several times in search of higher pay (Life Saving Service wages were meager at best). But he always returned, starting over as a Surfman and again rising to the rank of Keeper somewhere along the Lake Superior shore.

In the fall of 1912, Ocha transferred to be the first Keeper at the new, Eagle Harbor Station. He left behind the graves of his wife and several of his children at his last post, the Big Two-Heart River. He was poor. Unable to afford a wagon to haul his possessions and remaining children the distance to Eagle Harbor, he built a flat bottomed barge and depended on the kindness of a friend to tow it all the way to his new post. He and his children rode in his own boat, a thirty-six-footer with a small, twelve-horsepower motor.

He arrived in Eagle Harbor in mid-October, 1912 and barely a month later, at the age of 49, he died of liver complications aggravated by the strain of moving, opening the station and training a new crew. Life Savers from across Lake Superior turned out for his funeral and he was buried in the Eagle Harbor Cemetery. However, due to his financial situation, his grave was modestly marked, if at all. Any traces of where the great hero of Lake Superior lies buried, have been long claimed by the harsh weather of the lake herself.

Albert Ocha spent most of his life battling the forces of Lake Superior and in the end, it was Superior who claimed the last physical trace of his existence. However, the legends that heroes be... live forever.

To learn more about the Life Saving Service in the Great Lakes, please enjoy *Wreck Ashore,* by Frederick Stonehouse. I would like to personally thank Mr. Stonehouse for his help in researching this story.

The Lights Of The Apostles

You may already know that the greatest concentration of lighthouses anywhere in the world is right here in the Great Lakes. But did you know that the greatest concentration of lighthouses in the Great Lakes is in the Apostle Islands? It's a fact! In this relatively small area of western-most Lake Superior, there are no less than six classic lighthouses that you can enjoy in one fashion or another.

Why so many? There's really a very simple answer... they were needed. Bayfield was a fast growing lake port in the mid-1800s. The first lock in the Soo Canal system had just opened and shipping traffic on Lake Superior was growing by leaps and bounds. Bayfield had much to offer the world in the form of lumber, fish and other natural resources and much of that cargo was shipped by water. Schooners and steamers were once a regular part of the village skyline as boats loaded and unloaded at the pier.

However, the naturally beautiful scenery of the Apostle Islands was a navigator's nightmare... especially after dark. A system of navigational aids, (lighthouses), was built over the years. There was no grand, master plan that called for this many lights. The entire "collection" of lights grew over time as needs became evident.

The first light was built in 1857 on the shore of Michigan Island. This was a mistake, literally or allegedly, as the light was granted by Congress to be built as the LaPort Light across from LaPort on Long Island, guiding the ships into Bayfield through the South Channel. How it wound up quite some distance away on Michigan Island is a mystery to this day. Was the contractor *that* confused over local geography? Seeing that most lighthouses were built by local contractors to government specifications, this seems unlikely. Did someone on Michigan Island have a parcel of land they wanted to get rid of at a good, government price? Possibly. Either way, a very nice, stucco lighthouse, similar to others in the Great Lakes, was built there.

The very next year, when the mistake was noted, the Michigan Island light was decommissioned and a lighthouse built at the appropriate site on Long Island. There are no records showing any more funds allocated for its construction. Looking at the original structure, a simple, wooden-framed house with a wooden tower, it is suspected that the contractor had to build this lightstation out of his own pocket, having been paid in full for the "mistake."

Several years later, congress was petitioned and moved to reopen the light on Michigan Island as the shipping trade continued to grow. Since there was a lighthouse already there, they didn't have to pay to have this one built. The government got two lighthouses for the cost of one, and the contractor would have eventually been paid to build two lighthouses, if he had done it right the first time. I guess that's just one of those little quirks of fate we call history.

In another historical footnote, the Fresnel lens from the Michigan Island Light (it was upgraded to more modern equipment when the beacon was moved to a nearby skeleton tower), is on display in the Apostle Islands National Park Visitors center in downtown Bayfield. Actually, this is the lighthouse's second lens. The very first lens, the one that was put there by accident, was moved to Detroit's Windmill Point Lighthouse on Lake St. Clair, when the Michigan Island light was closed in 1858.

When the light was re-commissioned in 1869, a new lens was installed at that time. This is the lens on display in Bayfield. Several other lighthouses followed as the 19th Century progressed. Today, all of these lights are still here and are all on the National Registry Of Historic Places. Several of the lights have wonderfully maintained grounds and make great photo opportunities. Some have volunteer tour guides to show you around.

Two highlights not to miss: The Sand Island lighthouse is built of locally quarried brownstone and shows some "liberal interpretation" of the government's stringent lighthouse blueprints.

This one is more Gothic than Victorian! Also don't miss the Raspberry Island Lighthouse as this one is open as a museum complete with costumed tour guides who do a fantastic job of "time travel." From the minute you step on the grounds, you will have to keep reminding yourself that this is the 21st century, not the late 1800s. That's how good the staff is at recreating the daily life of "the keeper of the light on Raspberry Island..."

The Ontonagen Boulder

The area in and surrounding Ontonagon is historically, one of the most important pieces of real estate in Michigan's Upper Peninsula. It has been many things to many people, but from the very first, it belonged to the Native Americans, specifically the Chippewa.

As near as we can ascertain, the Ontonagon area was high holy ground to the Chippewa tribe. After all, who could have created such beauty, such plentiful hunting grounds, such needed resources all in one area, but a God? The name Ontonagon itself is a Chippewa word spelled many ways over as many years but still meaning the same thing: "I've lost my bowl" or "place of the lost bowl." Those who are more learned in the ways of Native Americans than I admit they can only guess at the origin of such a name, but they did have several keen insights that could at least point us in a likely direction.

It is unlikely that such a place would acquire and then retain a name such as "I've lost my bowl" based on the experience of a common tribe member. It would more likely have to be a quotation from a Chief or Princess, or perhaps a medicine man or religious leader. The point is it would have to be someone in high social standing in the tribe and then the loss of the bowl would need to be a significant event in the course of the tribe's history. Most likely, the person who lost the bowl would have to be the most powerful person in the tribe's existence ... such as a deity.

Native American religion and folk lore are generally unique in the way the Gods interact with mere humans. Most European Gods, from the Greeks, the Romans and the Norsemen have Gods that are of supernatural size and power when on their mountain tops or riding their chariots across the sky. Yet, when they found it necessary to deal with mortal man on a face to face basis, they always took a proportional size and form.

Native American Gods often retained their size and stature when dealing with man. Their history is rich with stories where the tears of a Goddess in the sky filled a lake, or the hand of an angered deity flattened a great plain. Is it not unreasonable to believe then that a larger than life Goddess could drop her bowl from somewhere in the heavens, and that it might land near the mouth of the Ontonagon River forming a great, circular shaped natural harbor? And what better place for this miracle to happen than in the midst of hallowed ground? It's one explanation, one of several possibilities.

To help support that theory is the reality of the Ontonagon Boulder. Discovered (by the White Man) in 1767, the famous boulder was an ingot of pure Copper naturally occurring in the Ontonagon River. There were large deposits of nearly pure Copper and there was evidence that the natives had been mining this metal for religious and decorative purposes for generations.
But the Ontonagon Boulder was truly special. It is still today, the largest single copper "nugget" ever found. Don't think baseball, football or even basketball-sized. Think, 'small automobile-sized!'

It was also a religious icon to the Chippewa people. Through it, by virtue of its size and purity, they spoke to their God. And evidently, many people of the Chippewa tribe would travel to the Ontonagon area to do just that.

But the white man pushed west. After the war of 1812 when secure control of all the five Great Lakes fell into American hands, there was a new wave of settlement and civilization that came into what was then called the Northwest Territory. The Ontonagon Boulder was safe, only because it was on land that had not been ceded over by the natives.

I find it hard to believe that there was one Chippewa alive at the time who felt it was a good idea, but in 1842, with white settlers already taking up residence in the area, the lands surrounding the Ontonagon River were signed over to the U.S. Government.

In short order, the Ontonagon Boulder was moved to the mouth of the river and removed by boat. Within a year, the instrument the Chippewa used to talk to their God was on display in Detroit for two bits a peek. Eventually, it wound up in the Smithsonian Institute where it remains to this day, under the protection of the Great White Father, never having been returned to its rightful owners.

The Legend Of
The Sleeping Giant

In northern Lake Superior is the small city of Thunder Bay, Ontario. Long before this was a modern shipping port, there were First Nation settlements here stretching back before recorded history. The suitability of this shoreline has to do with the protected waters of Thunder Bay, shielded from the open lake by the Sibley Peninsula. However, the peninsula also held one of the richest silver mines in North America. From a distance, the natural formed mesas on the peninsula look like a giant man, laying on his back in the water. It is certainly this similarity that, in part, gave rise to the legend of the sleeping giant.

As Native North American legends go, that of the Sleeping Giant is relatively recent and actually references European settlement along the shores of the Great Lakes. It is really an interesting legend, and one that for all practical reasons, should make you pause and reflect even today.

Nanabosho, the great giant, was the protector of the Ojibwe people. He led them to this bountiful peninsula so that they might prosper and, be protected from their terrible enemy, the Sioux. One day, while sitting on the shore of this great water, Nanabosho scratched a rock and beneath its surface, discovered silver! Silver was worthless to the Ojibwe people, but Nanabosho knew it would bring the White Man in great numbers and they would lose this land.

He ordered his people to bury the silver on the tiny island at the southern end of the Peninsula and made them swear, never to reveal its whereabouts. But all men can be human and humans can be vain. One of the Chieftains succumbed to temptation and fashioned himself a most glorious weapon from the silver and carried it into battle against the Sioux. But this battle was his last and the Sioux found the silver weapon next to his fallen body.

A few days later, Nanabosho watched a Sioux warrior canoeing his way across the lake, heading towards the peninsula. With him were two White Men, one carrying the fallen chieftain's silver weapon.

The Great Spirit forbid Nanabosho to interfere, but the giant loved his people more and raised a great storm on the lake, drowning the men in the canoe. As punishment, the Great Spirit turned Nanabosho to stone, and there, he sleeps today, at the very foot of the peninsula he saved for the Ojibwe people.

Please note, the legend refers to a *sleeping* giant, not a dead one. No one knows for how long the giant is supposed to sleep. The legend gives no prophecy as to when the Great Spirit might awaken Nanabosho. Just always remember, Nanabosho had sworn to protect this land from the White Man and the first two that came here, he drowned. So when the storm seas boil and the shoals reach out for your hull, ask yourself, how soundly is the giant sleeping tonight?

The Long Way Home:
The Story Of The *Ella Ellenwood*

Back before the turn of the century, the 157 ton lumber schooner, *Ella Ellenwood* was the pride of the community of White Lake (today, known as the sister cities of Montague and White Hall, Michigan). On regular runs, she would take the harvest of the local sawmills to the furthest corners of Lake Michigan, and then she would triumphantly return home with the bounty and profits her cargo had won. So many times the local citizenry had looked up from their labors to see this proud vessel churning her way through a morning mist as she set out for the open waters of Lake Michigan. And just as often, they had seen her rigging full of sailors searching the shore for loved ones upon her return home. The *Ella Ellenwood* was swift, safe, and most of all, she was theirs.

But in late September, 1901, the *Ella Ellenwood* set her sails and left the safety of White Lake for the very last time. On the night of October 1st, she found herself struggling for her very life in a strong northeastern gale that had blown down from Canada. The crew desperately tried to hold their own in the face of the building storm but eventually found themselves hard aground on the shoals near Fox Point just 8 miles northeast of the protected harbor in Milwaukee. They tried to free her, then to save her, but when it was clear that all was lost, they were forced to abandon her in the yawl. The crew was saved but the *Ella Ellenwood* was a total loss. Her crew watched as the fury of the storm literally pounded the pride of White Lake to pieces before the larger sections of her hull were swept from the reef and slid into the depths below.

It was a long winter that year in the twin cities of Montague and Whitehall. Perhaps it wasn't the weather as much as the loss of the *Ella Ellenwood* that made the season so cold, but whatever the reason, most of the local citizenry mourned the loss of their lumber schooner as if she were a member of their own family. Thinking of her never coming home again was difficult indeed.

Then, in the spring of 1902, when the ice finally cleared the channel that connects Lake Michigan with White Lake, they made a startling discovery. A board. A board that when pulled from the channel proved to be a section of the nameplate from the lost schooner's bow. She *had* made her way home, the best she could.

Today, the craft is immortalized in brass atop the giant wind vane that once stood in the harbor, but has since been moved to the corner of Water and Dowling Streets in the heart of the village of Montague. And depending on who you talk to, you might also get a glimpse of her through an early morning fog, churning her way through the waves towards the open waters of Lake Michigan.

The Mailman

Over a hundred years ago, along the northwest shore of Lake Superior, there was little you could depend on. You could *never* depend on the weather, and since the weather controlled just about everything else, well… Would the steamers arrive today? Would the ore or the lumber get down to the docks on time? Would the train arrive, at all? Everything revolved on these events and it made everything else in life, less-than-dependable.

Unless you were talking about the U.S. Mail, that is. Back in the late 1800s, much of the mail around these parts was delivered, much of the year, by dog sled team. And if you could depend on anything, it was that the mail would be there, and probably early at that.

This was all due to the efforts, the determination, and the dedication of one man: John Beargrease. His dog sled skills were legendary, his team incomparable, and what he gave to the people of the North Shore was priceless. The mail brought them hope, contact, a reason to suffer through some of the worst storms on the continent. But no matter what the weather, John Beargrease brought the news of loved ones they needed so dearly.

In modern times, a full century after John Beargrease delivered his last letter, there is a celebration. Every January marks the running of the John Beargrease Sled Dog Marathon. Dog sled teams from near and far line up for the long-distance race from Duluth to Grand Portage on the Canadian border and back, with layovers in Two Harbors. It's a total distance of some five hundred miles. The dogs and their drivers suffer through the worst a Lake Superior winter can throw at them, through snow and sleet and darkest nights… and all in memory, of a mailman.

The Masseys In Ontario, Or, "You Can Call Me Ray..."

The Massey family first came to the New World from England in 1630. Over the generations that followed, they migrated west and north to the New York shores of Lake Ontario. Around 1802, Daniel Massey Sr., his wife and infant son, Daniel, migrated from Watertown, New York, across the lake to the Canadian shore. Here he staked-out a 200-acre homestead and began clearing the land for farming.

Young Daniel was sent back to Watertown to live with his grandparents when he was just six-years-old and as he grew up, he made many trips between the two settlements. By the time he was 21, he was an accomplished entrepreneur. He had already purchased his own 200 acres next to his parents farm and was rapidly acquiring more land and hired hands to clear and work it. His financial interests included lumbering as well as agricultural holdings.

Eventually, he began bringing machinery and tools in from the American side and putting them to work on his Canadian farmland. Among the first was the 'Bull Thresher' which was set up in the Massey barn and was so efficient, neighboring farmers were soon bringing their grain to Massey for threshing. Since the nearest blacksmith was some distance away, Daniel Massey established a machine shop to be used by himself and his neighbors for the maintenance and repair of their tools and equipment. Soon, Massey's interests were more in the shop than on the farm and he turned over his farming interests to his son so he could spend more time with the machines.

Leave a creative man alone with tools in the middle of the Industrial Revolution and you shouldn't be surprised with what happens. In short order, he was designing and building his own farming equipment. In 1847, he needed larger quarters and formed a partnership with a Richard Vaughn in nearby Newcastle Village. The business grew rapidly and within a year, Massey bought out Vaughn and was already looking for larger quarters in town.

To make a long story shorter, the business of manufacturing farm equipment (in those days, horse-drawn plows, stump pullers, harrows and so on), prospered in this economically developing heartland and over time, Massey's son, Hart and other generations of Massey men came into the family business. Factories and shops were built, staffed, supervised and families built homes and grew within their walls.

In 1862 the company (then called the Newcastle Agricultural Works) printed and distributed its first catalog. By 1863, they couldn't keep up with the orders and the business and its facilities expanded again. In 1866, they demonstrated their products at the Toronto Industrial Exhibition and were chosen to represent Canadian manufacturing at the International Exhibition in Paris, France, the next year. In Paris, in the field trials, the Massey Self Binder harvested an entire section of oats two and a half times faster than their nearest competitor, and soon, international orders began pouring in to the Newcastle headquarters.

1878 was a critical year for the company. This was the year they introduced their new Massey Harvester, a completely Canadian design and a major step forward in farm automation. The Masseys planned to build an unheard of, 200 units of this new machine. Shortly after introduction, they were swamped with 500 orders! Even though men worked day and night shifts, they were unable to meet demand and the manufacturing facility was forced to move to Toronto where larger manufacturing facilities, a larger labor pool and ample supplies of raw materials could be found.

This proved hard times for the people of Newcastle but the Masseys never forgot their hometown. Many of the public buildings and churches were built with Massey money including the Community Hall still at the corner of Mill and King Streets in the center of the village.

In the years that followed, more generations of Massey men joined the family business as it continued to grow and prosper. In 1891, Massey Manufacturing joined with A. Harris, Son & Company to form Massey-Harris and in 1953, they merged with Harry Ferguson to become Massey-Harris-Ferguson, shortened in 1957 to just Massey-Ferguson, the world's premier manufacturer of agricultural machinery.

But not all Massey men had fit so well into the family business. One of Chester Massey's sons didn't seem to have much interest in the family manufacturing business at all. In fact, for whatever strange reasons, he felt he could contribute more to the world on the stage and set off to become an actor of all things. He didn't do too badly, though. He won an Oscar for his portrayal of Abraham Lincoln in 'Abe Lincoln Of Illinois.' Of course I'm not talking about Vincent Massey, Chester's son who became the first Canadian-born Governor General of all Canada, I'm talking about his other son, Raymond Massey.

The Oakland Hotel

Not far south of the AKZO Salt Plant in St. Clair, Michigan, you'll come to two very important structures along the St. Clair River bank. One is the St. Clair Post of the Michigan State Police. Next to it, a bait and tackle shop known as the Angler Rod & Sports. What do fishing tackle and State Troopers have in common? They have both taken up residence on the former site of the famed Oakland Hotel. To replace one of the "grandest of the grand," this must be one important tackle shop and a most impressive Police Post. But we're getting ahead of ourselves. We'd better start by rolling back the clock over one hundred years.

In brief, local millwright and pipe joiner, Samuel Hopkins was fortunate enough to have an extremely wealthy brother, who lived a shorter life than Samuel. The brother, Mark Hopkins, had made his fortune first in the gold rush (he was not a prospector, he sold mining supplies to prospectors!), and then in the transcontinental railroad. When he died in 1879, he left his entire estate, worth more than twenty million dollars, to his brother and his brother's children. Samuel's son, also named Mark, took over most of the family finances and soon put this vast fortune to work improving the lives and the livelihoods of the local residents.

Amongst several business investments the family made, was the construction of the luxurious Oakland Hotel on the site of a small mineral spring. In the late Victorian Era, mineral springs were generally believed to be the magic cure for most any ailment. Of course, mineral springs tended to be in remote areas, and extended stays were the standard course of treatment. This meant that such cures were really only accessible to the wealthy.

So, the doctors prescribed a month in the magic waters and the rich Victorian industrialists would pack up their families, leave the polluted air of the coal-burning factories and the stress of their six-day work weeks, and head for the mineral springs. Of course, in keeping with their guests, the hotels near these health-giving waters tended to be more than just comfortable… they were downright elegant, opulent and the most luxurious facilities you could imagine.

Of course, taking a month in the clean country air, away from the daily stress, away from that telephone thing, basking in the sun and playing croquet on the manicured lawn tended to have very positive effects on the health of the guests. But should you ask anyone, it was without a doubt, the magic in the minerals in the water! The Oakland Hotel was no exception.

This grand resort was among the most luxurious in the Great Lakes. She was two-hundred and thirty five feet long, four stories high and constructed entirely of wood. Huge covered verandahs stretched out from the first and third floors and the entire structure was nestled into the hillside on the banks of the river. Below, the Oakland's private docks awaited those wealthy guests who arrived by luxury steamer, or, if you preferred rail travel, the hotel's own rail terminal sat on the southern edge of the property.

Inside, guests were pampered in private suites that rivaled the *Titanic*, complete with marble fireplace mantles and Brussels carpets. There were approximately one-hundred and fifteen such rooms, ranging in price from $3 to $5 per day, the very same price charged by the Grand Hotel on Mackinac Island in the same era.

But the Oakland was also a complete resort with grass tennis courts, a riding stable, a gymnasium, a two-hundred acre woods with hiking trails and picnic grounds, fishing facilities and several other more mundane pastimes including a private bowling alley and billiard parlor. The Oakland had something for everyone.

But times and people change. Eventually telephone lines were installed so busy industrialists could keep in touch with their factories. The Interurban Railroad extended its line making commuting to and from the hotel a possibility for those just too busy to "just pack up and go." Then came the automobile so that guests could come and go as they wished… or as they needed.

Then, the strangest thing happened. The magic waters seemed to lose some of their magic. A month at the resort no longer seemed to have the positive effect it once did. Occupancy dropped. Soon, the hotel was only open during the height of the season and then, in 1915, it partially burned and didn't have the strength to recover.

The Oakland was closed and in the late 1920s, was demolished and removed from the river bank in the name of progress. The land was sold off for private residences, of which there are plenty in the area. But the heart of the hotel, the center of the resort is now occupied by the two aforementioned establishments. Someone should call the police…

Wreck Of The Gunilda

Shortly after the turn-of-the-century, William Lamont Harkness inherited his father's fortune of some thirty-seven million dollars. This was a tidy sum, especially back then. It left the younger Mr. Harkness free to pursue his favorite pastime, yachting. He owned several but his pride and joy, was the *Gunilda.*

She was the ultimate statement in luxury and unconstrained wealth. She was one-hundred and ninety-eight feet overall, a graceful, white-hulled beauty with gold leaf inlay around her name plate and other conspicuous areas. Her living quarters were decorated with the finest framed tapestries, hand-woven rugs, sterling silver and bone china. Rare books and art objects were also said to be in abundance on board.

In 1910, Harkness brought his precious *Gunilda* into the Great Lakes for a summer cruise. So taken by the beauty of the inland seas, he vowed to return the next summer for an extended trip along the rugged north shore of Lake Superior. True to his word, he was near Rossport, Ontario about mid-summer, 1911, with his wife and children, and other friends along.

One day, they were taking on coal and supplies at Jack Fish Bay when the Captain of the *Gunilda* decided it was best to hire a local pilot to help guide them through the rocky islands and shoals of Nipigon Bay. He had never sailed these waters before and only had American charts, not Canadian charts on board. He had negotiated with a local named Harry LeGault to ride along with them for the fee of $15, plus another $10 for his train fare back to Jack Fish.

When Harkness got wind of this, he was outraged. They had charts and a competent crew on board. He felt the sum was outrageous and a complete waste of $25. They set off without Harry LeGault.

Upon entering the bay, the American charts showed a good three-hundred feet of water beneath them and the captain ordered full speed ahead in order to reach a prime anchorage by the end of the day. But shortly into the run, they encountered something that wasn't on the American charts: McGarvey Shoal.

The yacht hit the granite rock with a tremendous shock and her momentum carried her up, out of the water to where the bow was high and dry and pointed skyward, and her stern portholes were barely two feet above the waters of Nipigon Bay. Miraculously, she had suffered little damage and was not taking on water! She was indeed, soundly built. If she could be pulled off the rocks, she would float and minor repairs could be made at a harbor of choice.

The guests and extraneous crew were evacuated, the insurance company notified, and in time, a salvage crew arrived to attempt to re-float the *Gunilda*. However, upon viewing the yacht, the salvage captain, one of the most experienced in the lakes, felt the need for additional barges to give lift to the *Gunilda's* stern. As she came off the rock, he feared she might take a serious list one way or the other.

But again, Harkness wouldn't hear of it. This was yet just another example of how everybody was always trying to run up his bills and charge him more than was necessary, just because he was rich. He said that she went on straight, she'll come off straight, and gave the order to proceed with the operation.

With great effort and after several tries, the tugs finally got the great yacht to move back off the rock, but after a few feet, the *Gunilda* did the expected and listed hard to starboard. This angle put her starboard stern rail below the water. It seems that in their haste to refloat and in anticipation of an easy recovery, no one had thought to close any of the stern portholes or seal any of the bulkheads.

The yacht immediately began to flood at an uncontrollable rate. As her bow climbed higher in the sky, there was nothing for the tug captains to do but cut the tow lines so that they didn't follow her to the bottom. Progressively, geysers burst out her portholes up the length of the ship and it was all over in a few minutes. She slipped beneath the surface of Nipigon Bay and settled, upright, on the rocky bottom, some three-hundred feet below.

As she disappeared from sight, Mr. Harkness was heard to sheepishly say to the salvage captain: "Well, they're still building others like her..."

About the Author

Bruce Jenvey was raised in rural Michigan with a great interest in history, popular culture and the paranormal. After twenty years in the advertising industry, he founded *Great Lakes Cruiser Magazine* and spent the next decade traveling the region as both historian and journalist.

Along the way, Bruce had unique access to untold incidents and documentation of the unexplained. He collected and chronicled these experiences in every place he found them, from the shores of Lake Michigan to Upstate New York. As he did so, he was struck by how consistent and similar these accounts were from region to region leading him to the conclusion that all we see, may *not* be all there is to know...

Today, Bruce is the award-winning author of *Angela's Coven,* and the Cabbottown Witch Novels as well as other tales of the paranormal. Visit our site for the latest releases in digital and paperback:

www.covenbooks.com

Made in United States
Orlando, FL
09 April 2023